EURON GRIFFITH
THE BEATLES IN TONYPANDY

Euron Griffith was born in Bangor, North Wales. At the earliest opportunity he ran away to the University of Kent to study English and to concentrate on growing his hair to ridiculous lengths. Boldly deciding to either be a great writer or starve, he rapidly became intimately familiar with the location of every bin in Canterbury. Desperate, he got a proper job with the BBC. He now lives with three cats and a goldfish in a very tense Victorian house in Cardiff.

EURON GRIFFITH

THE BEATLES IN TONYPANDY

DEAN STREET PRESS

Published by Dean Street Press 2017

Copyright © 2017 Euron Griffith

All Rights Reserved

The right of Euron Griffith to be identified as the Author of the Work has been asserted by him in accordance with the Copyright, Designs and Patents Act 1988.

'The Beatles in Tonypandy' first published in *In My Life: Encounters with the Beatles* (Fromm International, 1996), and later in *Ambit* magazine (2008)

'Dylan Goes Electric' first published in *Iron* magazine (1999)

'A Digression Regarding the Dangers of Excessive Hospitality' first published in *Sing Sorrow, Sorrow* (Seren Books, 2010)

'Theme Park' first published in *Teaching a Chicken to Swim* (Seren Books, 2000)

'Villa Nellcote' first published in Welsh in *Clymau* (Gomer Press, 2015), here translated by the author

'Short Cut' first published in *New Welsh Review* (1995)

'The Sad Tale of "Crazy" Luke Dober' and 'Hanes Trist "Crazy" Luke Dober' first published in Welsh in *Leni Tiwdor* (Y Lolfa, 2013), here translated by the author

Cover by DSP
ISBN 978 1 911579 15 1

www.deanstreetpress.co.uk

CONTENTS

I
THE BEATLES IN TONYPANDY *1*

II
DYLAN GOES ELECTRIC *25*

III
A DIGRESSION REGARDING THE DANGERS OF EXCESSIVE HOSPITALITY (AND THE LEGENDARY UNPREDICTABILITY OF THE WASP) *53*

IV
THEME PARK *69*

V
VILLA NELLCÔTE *101*

VI
SHORT CUT *117*

VII
THE SAD TALE OF "CRAZY" LUKE DOBER *133*

VIII
HANES TRIST "CRAZY" LUKE DOBER *153*

"THE BEATLES ARE COMING!"
AN AFTERWORD *173*

I

THE BEATLES IN TONYPANDY

I

IN 1967, a mere twelve weeks before they flew out to Rishikesh with the Maharishi, the Beatles came to Tonypandy, South Wales, and spent six days with Tom Morris of 23 Upper Chemical Terrace.

Up until now the details of what occurred during these six days have remained something of a magical mystery for Beatles scholars but, following Tom's death last year, important papers, letters and tapes were recently put up for auction at Sotheby's by Tom's widow Eileen and, as a result of their purchase by Professor Remi Carne of

UCLA we are now, with Professor Carne's kind permission, able at last to throw some light on what went on in that tiny terraced house.

II

It has not yet been possible to establish with any certainty how the Beatles came to be aware of Tom Morris and his pigeons, although Gannon and McCall have suggested that it could have been through an article in the *Sunday Times* from August 28, 1966 entitled "Tom Morris – A Man And His Birds". However, Mark Sammon's conviction that the Beatles were made aware of Tom Morris through one of his talks – "Pigeons And Their Ways" – was confirmed this year with the historic publication of the Tom Morris diaries. According to one entry, Morris first met the Beatles at a talk he gave to the Kent Pigeon Society at Maidstone's Memorial Hall on September 23, 1967. The Beatles at this time were filming additional scenes for *Magical Mystery Tour* at nearby West Malling and it was through a suggestion made by one of the extras that Paul McCartney and Ringo Starr decided to attend Morris's lecture. The entry for that date makes it obvious that Morris had no idea who these two young men were.

5 | THE BEATLES IN TONYPANDY

Saturday 23rd.

Caught 09.05 from Cardiff to Paddington. Got lost on tube but eventually got connection. Arrived at Maidstone. Nice spread laid out by Society – chicken sandwiches and hot sausage rolls. Met Ken, the chairman – lovely fellow, said he'd done some of his National Service in Wales. Met Lynne, his lovely lady wife. Complimented her on the sausage rolls. At their house was impressed with micromesh netting system. The pigeons love it apparently. Must make enquiries at Jepson's on reaching Ton. Gave talk. Halfway through two young men came in. Both long-haired. One had v. big nose. Expected the worst but both sat down and listened intently. At the end they asked lots of questions about pigeons. Invited me to their hotel but politely declined. Gave them my address back in Ton. Said if they needed more information they were welcome to correspond. They thanked me and left. Kent seemed v. excited. "Fancy that," he kept saying, "who'd have believed it?" "Yes," I said, "nice to know that not every young man these days is obsessed with beat music and drugs." Got paid ten shillings and caught last train to London. Sore throat. Might have developed a late summer chill. Made a note to ring Dr Meredith on return.

It is obvious that Tom Morris's talk had an immediate effect on McCartney and Starr. Three days later (according to receipts which have recently been acquired by the Beatle Museum of Japan in Kyoto) they bought six pigeons from champion breeder Alf Baker of Wood Green at five pounds each. Problems began to arise however when it came to the subject of feeding. "We knew nothing really," said McCartney in a Radio 2 interview from last year. "At first we tried All-Bran and Ready Brek mixed with water but it was clear that the birds weren't happy. I phoned Ringo and both of us agreed that something had to be done otherwise we'd lose them."

Ringo in fact had even bigger problems. After a late-night session for *I Am the Walrus* he and John Lennon returned to Ringo's flat in Kensington and, on seeing the pigeons, Lennon fed them some sugar cubes laced with LSD. "They just went mad," said Ringo. "They literally cooed themselves to death." Maureen Starr, who was also present, remembered the occasion in her autobiography *My Life with Ringo*. "Very strange," she wrote. "One minute they were sitting on their perch and the next they just kind of dropped off. I think the acid must have convinced them that they couldn't fly."

It must have been at this time that McCartney wrote his first letter to Tom Morris. Unfortunately the document has not survived but Tom Morris's reply has, dated October 8, 1967.

Dear Mr McCartney,

Thank you for your letter. I'm glad that you enjoyed my little talk and I was glad also to learn of your new interest in pigeons. I was sorry to hear of your friend's mishap with his birds – I've never heard of pigeons being savaged by stray Alsatians before but I have been told, on many occasions, that keeping prize birds in a big city poses different kinds of problems.

With regard to your enquiries about feeding may I suggest that you and your friend try Haith's maize or Willsbridge? A twenty-eight pound bag of mixed corn, maize and wheat barley shouldn't cost you more than sixteen shillings. Alternatively, you could purchase a half-hundredweight bag at around one pound and seventeen shillings. Let me know how you get on. Must close now. It's settling up day at the Co-Op.

Yours,

Tom.

Ringo replaced his dead pigeons on October 10 and, according to Alf Baker's records, he and McCartney arranged for deliveries of half-hundredweight bags of mixed corn and maize to their respective addresses. These arrived on October 12 although, on this day, both Starr and McCartney were overdubbing *Blue Jay Way* at De Lane Lea Recording Studios in London.

After a couple of days Starr and McCartney were delighted to see that their pigeons were thriving on their new diet and they were also delighted with their newly-arrived membership cards for the Pigeon Fancier's Club Of Great Britain (McCartney's number was 012435B and Starr's was 012437B). The other two Beatles at this time were sceptical about pigeons. Harrison in particular appeared especially hostile and McGarry and Locke have indicated that this was probably due to his recent introduction to the Maharishi Mahesh Yogi. "That was George's thing," said McCartney. "And he was dead keen to turn us on to it. Me and John had been to a couple of his lectures in London but, even though he was a cool guy and everything we remained suspicious. Pigeons were straightforward by comparison. It was mind-blowing in a way but when you released a pigeon from your loft or from the back garden you got this real buzz. I got the riff for *Lady Madonna* whilst flying pigeons."

As a means of introducing Harrison to pigeons McCartney and Starr took him to the South Bucks

Meet on October 21. When Lennon arrived unexpectedly this must have been the first time that the Beatles, as a collective, interacted with what was to shortly become for them a door into a new universe. From a home movie shot on that day by Ringo (and currently in the possession of the late Neil Aspinall's estate) it is remarkable how Paul and Ringo had assimilated into this new culture. Their clothes that day are indicative of this. Whilst John and George are wearing kaftans, beads and bells, Ringo and Paul are already parading the Crombie coats, cloth caps and scarves which the other Beatles would soon adopt and which would become their fashion mode signifier for the next four months. At one point McCartney even lights up a pipe.

III

Marian Payne, in her famous study of Hispanic children of the Tenderloin district of San Francisco, coined the term Purified Grandfather Syndrome. Here, young children who had been nurtured and culturally defined within a rigidly urban environment were proved to be dislocated from direct parental influence through various factors. The unsettling pace of the children's development made it difficult for them to accept the authority of their parents. Their parents were too close. These children needed someone with distance, someone with a pre-media conception of reality. Their grandparents fitted the bill because their rural cultural instincts forged a valuable sense of balance in the social landscape of their disenfranchised grandchildren.

By September 1967 the Beatles were displaying many symptoms of Purified Grandfather Syndrome. Their gang mentality, forged through many years of touring and performing, had bereaved them of anything resembling a conventional form of social interaction and their considerable fame ensured that outside influences of any kind were extremely hard to assimilate. Like those children Payne described, the Beatles distrusted direct "parental" control. Indeed, the closest thing to a collective father figure they had – their manager Brian Epstein – had recently died and, as peripheral as he'd been in terms of his influence on the Beatles towards the end of his life, the Beatles no doubt found his loss alienating and disconcerting. It was natural in these circumstances therefore that the gang, childlike in its collective grieving, should search for a grandfather figure – someone who could instil the wisdom of a previous era and give them direction in a dark and troubled time. It is in this new light that we should perhaps see Tom Morris. In the end it could be argued that it was he who elevated the Beatles to a higher plane. Cast in the unconscious role of "grandfather" he kick-started a crucial process of self-examination and cosmic awareness in the group which would ultimately lead them to the Maharishi and the challenging ideas of the East.

It was Tom Morris who gave the Beatles back their sanity, not his pigeons. In the end his pigeons were nothing more than red herrings.

IV

Whether the Beatles were at all conscious of any symptoms of Purified Grandfather Syndrome, one thing is at least certain: they needed to see Tom Morris and their need was great enough to lure them out of their protected social pattern in London.

Up until the recent publication of the Tom Morris diaries, the exact nature and chronology of the Beatles' visit to Tonypandy has remained shrouded in mystery and somewhat open to speculation. Indeed, many Beatle scholars appeared unaware of any such visit in the first place. There is no mention of it in the mainstream biographies of Hunter Davies and Phillip Norman and Mark Lewisohn's otherwise exhaustive study of 1992 omits any reference to Tom Morris or to pigeons in general. Perhaps these shortcomings are pardonable, however, when we take into account the Beatles' unusually tight security during this visit. Unlike their previous trip to Wales (when they'd travelled from Euston Station, London to Bangor with the Maharishi on August 25, 1967) this time there were no press releases and no itinerary. As far as the world was concerned the Beatles were in the studio putting the final touches to the music for their television film *Magical Mystery Tour*. The visit to Tonypandy, although mentioned obliquely in interviews by the ex-Beatles since the mid-seventies, was only confirmed by the Apple office last year following Tom Morris's death, and it was only six months ago that the office offered any kind of explanation for the Beatles' military-style secrecy concerning the trip. It was done, according to the statement, "as a mark of respect for Tom. The boys didn't want Tom, or Eileen, to be hassled by the world's press and they didn't want his world – or his pigeons – to be crushed by the media circus." If news of the visit came as a surprise to certain Beatles scholars last year it was, according to the diary, as much of a surprise for Tom Morris himself at the time. Although he had entertained a healthy correspondence with the Beatles (and with Paul McCartney in particular) since his first meeting with Paul and Ringo in Maidstone, he was nevertheless astounded to find the four of them standing at the front door of 23 Chemical Terrace on the early evening of Saturday, November 11, 1967. An extract from Tom's diary entry for that day will confirm this.

> *Had tea and some of Eileen's lovely scones. Tried to take my mind off Brenda's legs. Two weeks now since the injury. Thought of taking her to the vet on Monday but dreading the verdict. Was just about to pick up the "Rhondda Leader" to try finishing the crossword when the doorbell went. Eileen said it was for me. Most surprised to find Paul and his young friends from London. Surprised also to find them dressed up as miners. John seemed to have boot polish rubbed into his face. They came in and had some tea. Asked if they could stay for a few days. Eileen was delighted. Ever since Ifan left home she's missed the company of young folk. She cleared out the spare room and brought down the tin bath in from the shed. She filled it up in the front room and bathed them one by one. I could tell it was the hard-bristled*

brush by their screams. She offered to cut their rather shaggy hair too but they said no. Later I showed them the loft and John helped me with the crossword. Very bright lad. Paul tuned the piano for Eileen and then we turned in. All in all a very eventful day.

The miners' hats and Davy lamps which the Beatles had rented two days earlier from Berry's Fancy Dress of Islington were intended as disguises but the group soon discovered that such precautions proved to be unnecessary on the streets of Tonypandy. Whereas during their touring days the Beatles had been forced to develop a fine instinct for camouflage in order to negotiate the streets of cities like London, New York and Los Angeles without provocation, they found that Tonypandy was refreshingly different. Here was a town which, in 1967, could only boast two fully-operational television sets. One was in the window of "Jenkins and Sons Radio Hire" and the other was the property of the Reverend Issac Eynon. Until the establishment of a new transmitter for the area in 1968, television reception in Tonypandy was notoriously poor. The set in the window of "Jenkins and Sons" showed nothing but constant interference and the Reverend Eynon's reasons for possessing a television set were a mystery for the entire town since he'd been blind from birth and, according to medical records, prone also to lengthy bouts of periodic deafness. His obituary in the *Rhondda Leader* in June 1971 records how he had often been forced "to yell out his sermons by braille".

In this media vacuum therefore, the Beatles were pleasantly surprised to discover that nobody appeared to recognize them. According to Tom Morris's diary entry for Sunday, November 12, his suggestion that they all "pop down to the Institute for a lunchtime pint" had initially provoked a visible air of apprehension in his young guests.

> *They got a bit tense and looked at each other as if I'd said something out of place. After a couple of minutes I threw on my coat and said "Look, I'm off. You're welcome to help Eileen in the kitchen if you want." With that they decided to come. I think they were scared of her since the bristled brush incident. They reached for their miners' hats and Davy lamps but I stopped them. "Don't be ridiculous," I said. "You'll only get folk staring at you if you wear those silly clothes." For some reason they all thought this was hilarious.*

At the Tonypandy Miners Institute the Beatles, for the first time since their pre-fame days in Hamburg, found themselves able to interact with people on a fairly normal everyday basis. "I couldn't believe it," said McCartney. "They'd obviously heard of the Beatles but I don't think anyone in Tonypandy had the vaguest idea what they looked like! To them we were just Tom's young friends from London who'd come to see his pigeons. Apparently he had a lot of visitors. He was quite a celebrity in pigeon circles."

The Beatles were especially drawn to the Institute and it's clear from Tom Morris's entry for Tuesday, November 14, that the group found it an easy place to relax.

Tuesday, November 14.

Knees-up night at the Institute. The boys came with me and Eileen. Ianto got up and played "She'll Be Coming Round the Mountain" on the piano and Dilys did the can-can as usual (really, I wish someone would have a word with her!). To my surprise Paul got up and sang "Yesterday" and, although we all applauded politely, I think that, privately, we all agreed that he was no Matt Monro. During the bingo John gave me one of his special Woodbines. Apparently they're all the rage in London with the young folk. I couldn't concentrate on my bingo after that. When Danny came on and told some jokes, even though I'd heard them all before, I embarrassed Eileen by laughing and giggling like a fool. Had chips on the way home. After Eileen had gone to bed John gave me another of his special Woodbines. In the morning I was surprised to discover that my shoes were on top of the coal shed.

From Eileen Morris's recollections of that period it is clear that key elements of Purified Grandfather Syndrome were consistently present in the Beatles relationship with Tom. "They were very close," she says. "One minute they were cleaning out the loft together and the next they were helping Tom carry big sacks of maize from the Davies Feed Warehouse. It wasn't just pigeons though. One day they went up to the hills to collect wild mushrooms. And then there was Dai of course. The boys were fascinated with him."

Dai, or David, Llewelyn was Tom and Eileen's next-door neighbour. A keen bird-watcher, he was also the proud owner of a Bush reel-to-reel tape recorder which he used to record the songs of wild birds in the area. "He carried this tape recorder with him everywhere," remembered Paul. "And this was very useful for John and me because we were inspired and new songs came out every day." (These tapes were discovered in Llewelyn's attic following his death in 1979. There were three reels in all, all of them labelled "Yellow Warbler" and they featured rough versions of songs which were later to appear on the *Beatles* double album of 1968. The tapes remain in the hands of the Llewelyn family but, in the presence of a solicitor, fragments of it were played to me in August 1995. What came over was the obvious joy in John and Paul's singing and writing. A version of *Ob-La-Di-Ob-La-Da* is improvised on Spanish guitar and washboard whilst a chaotic rendition of *Back in the USSR* is broken up when Eileen bangs the wall to tell them that their tea is ready. There follows a cascade of giggles before the tape runs out.)

The Beatles had temporarily escaped from the multi-faceted pressures of fame. Like the children in Marian Payne's study they had returned to the womb-like comfort of a predominantly rural generation and, in Tom Morris, they had found their symbolic "grandfather".

This idyllic state was shattered however, on the morning of Friday, November 17, 1967.

V

The Maharishi arrived in the Tonypandy coach depot on the 45 bus from Cardiff at 11.23 a.m.

How he came to be aware of the Beatles' precise whereabouts remains a mystery but he later claimed it was a karmic force which drew him to Wales. He took a taxi to Upper Chemical Terrace and knocked on the door of number 23.

"When I first opened the door," recalled Eileen, "I thought he was a Jehovah's Witness. I told him to go away but he had his foot in the door. 'Beetles,' he kept saying, 'you have beetles here?' 'Not anymore,' I said, 'the man from the council came last month – he got rid of them all.' But then Paul came up and they seemed to know each other so I let the man in. I don't think Paul was too happy to see him though. I know for a fact that Tom wasn't."

Tom's hostility towards the Maharishi Mahesh Yogi is evident from his diary entry for that day.

Friday, November 17.

That bloody man arrived! He sat in the lounge squeaking like a hamster and spreading Welsh cake crumbs everywhere. The boys looked uncomfortable. Poor old Ringo stared at me with those sad eyes and Paul kept running his hand through his hair nervously. John kept telling him he should have let them know he was coming. He said some rude things but the man didn't seem to mind – he just sat there grinning and laughing. Before John could hit him I suggested we go down the chip shop. I thought it might calm things down a bit. It was a big mistake.

The "Chip Shop Incident", as it has since been dubbed, has been outlined and reported by many Beatles scholars. Among the papers of Tom Morris however, a tape was discovered which was apparently recorded accidentally by Dai Llewelyn as he accompanied Tom, the Beatles and the Maharishi to Fat Ifan's Chip Emporium on the corner of Bryn Street and Caradoc Close. This tape (which also includes various recordings of thrushes and starlings) gives an invaluable insight into the events of that day. The full transcript – presented here for the first time – explains why the Beatles were forced to leave Tonypandy, and it also sheds some light on the mysterious story which appeared on the front page of the *Rhondda Leader* the following morning.

THE CHIP SHOP TAPE – A TRANSCRIPT

JOHN: What do you want then?

PAUL: Eh?

JOHN: What do you fucking want? You deaf or what?

PAUL: No, it's just that I ...

(Paul's answer is obscured by passing bus)

MAHARISHI: Well, I'd like a pasty.

FAT IFAN: Pasty and chips is it mate?

JOHN: Hang on, you can't have a pasty!

MAHARISHI: Why not? I have the money.

FAT IFAN: Three and six it is.

JOHN: Pasty and chips. Three and six. It's on the board over there.

RINGO: I'll have a pasty and chips please.

FAT IFAN: Right you are mate.

(Sound of chips frying)

MAHARISHI: And me please.

JOHN: But you're supposed to be a fucking vegetarian!

MAHARISHI: I eat goats.

JOHN: You what?

MAHARISHI: Goats and rice.

PAUL: What, goat curry?

MAHARISHI: Oh yes. With peas pulao and a side dish of mushroom thali. Very tasty.

FAT IFAN: I can get you some curry sauce if you like mate.

GEORGE: I'll have some of that.

FAT IFAN: Righto.

MAHARISHI: And a chips with a pasty.

FAT IFAN: Don't worry, I haven't forgotten.

MAHARISHI: With a pickled onion.

JOHN: You're going to be a fat Maharishi if you're not careful Maharishi.

(Maharishi giggles)

FAT IFAN: And what about you Tom? Usual is it? And a meat pie for the missus?

(Sound of a sudden scuffle)

UNKNOWN VOICE: Bloody hell ... it's them!
PAUL: Who the hell –
UNKNOWN VOICE: It's the sodding Beatles!
PAUL: Let's get out of here!

(There is considerable distortion and tape disruption at this point)

FAT IFAN: Hey, come back! Who's going to pay for all this food?

(Tape ends)

We can now confirm that the unidentified voice at the end of the tape belonged to Sam Fowler of the *Rhondda Leader*. Stopping by chance for some fish and chips with his photographer Lenny Tudor, he'd stumbled upon one of the major scoops in the paper's history. Unfortunately, in his excitement, Lenny Tudor dropped his camera in the middle of the road and, as he tried to retrieve it, he was struck unconscious by a Mini Moke.

The Beatles (and a by now no doubt totally confused Tom Morris) dashed down Upper Chemical Terrace and the hapless Fowler was left standing outside the chip shop.

The following day's edition of the *Rhondda Leader* carried a story of how the Beatles had been spotted on the streets of Tonypandy. Without photographs however it failed to be taken seriously. Fowler returned to Tonypandy on the afternoon of Saturday, November 18 but by then the Beatles and the Maharishi were on their way to London.

They never returned to Wales.

VI

Whether Tom Morris, his pigeons or his "self-contained social context" had any tangible benefits for the Beatles is almost impossible to calculate, but it is interesting to speculate whether he served as a catalyst for a new maturity in their lives and music.

By the spring of 1968 the Beatles were in Rishikesh, India with the Maharishi but Tom Morris had not been forgotten. The gratitude the Beatles felt was reflected in a postcard which arrived at Upper Chemical Terrace on February 23, 1968.

Dear Tom,

As you can see we're in India. It's hot as hell and Ringo's complaining about the food. Hope you and Eileen are well. Sorry we had to leave so suddenly that day – I'll explain it to you sometime. Thanks a lot for what you did. I don't think you know what you did but thanks anyway.

Best wishes from us all, love, Paul

The postcard remained on Tom Morris's mantelpiece until the day of his death.

II

DYLAN GOES ELECTRIC

THE MAN from *Time* magazine was used to being kept waiting. Two days for Cagney, six weeks for Astaire. He knew the score. What did they know or care about deadlines or final layout meetings? All they cared about was seeing their faces on the cover. So, for something like the hundredth time, the man from *Time* sighed and kicked his heels in a hallway. At least the location was new. The London Dorchester.

Twenty yards down the corridor, behind an elegant pair of leather-padded double doors, lay the eight hundred bucks a night Churchill Suite. Two lounges, four bedrooms, a bathroom with sauna and Jacuzzi, a fully stocked bar, two colour televisions and air-con. England was catching up, that was for sure.

The anxious-looking secretary cursed her typewriter. Aware of his gaze she looked up and flashed one of those cute half-smiles English girls did so well. He smiled back and focused on the leather-padded double doors.

It had been half an hour since they'd last been opened. On that occasion a tall woman with a beehive hairdo had appeared. She'd closed the doors gently behind her and walked on liquid hips to the secretary's desk. From a folder she pulled out some sheets of paper and placed them beside the typewriter.

"Quick as you can Sandra," she'd said.

He remembered her professional smile.

"Shouldn't be long now Mr Martinez."

Martinez had smiled back and watched as she opened the double-doors. A hint of light, a suggestion of furniture. And then it was gone.

The secretary gave a sigh of relief. She ripped the paper from the typewriter and placed it on top of the others at the side of the desk. She reached into her handbag and checked her hair and lipstick in a compact mirror before putting on her coat. As she tucked in her chair she turned to Martinez.

"I'm going for a sandwich. Would you like me to get you anything?"

"No thanks sweetheart. You go ahead. I'm fine."

He waited for a full minute before walking up to the desk. He picked up one of the newly-typed sheets and began to read.

> May 6th. Birmingham Trade Hall.
> Time of arrival: 6.00 pm
> Time of sound-check: 6.30 pm
> SHOWTIME: 7.30 pm
> Exit: 10.30 pm

> May 7th. Manchester Free Trade Hall.
> Time of arrival: 6.00 pm
> Time of sound-check: 6.30 pm
> SHOWTIME: 7.30 pm
> Exit: 10.30 pm (NB Meet Lord Mayor's wife and sons at 7.00)

> May 8th. Liverpool Empire –

The double-doors opened and the woman with the beehive re-appeared.

"Mr Martinez? We're ready for you now if you'd care to follow me."

He picked up his briefcase and walked through the leather-padded double doors into the Churchill Suite.

Martinez wasn't new to luxury suites; he'd interviewed Jayne Mansfield in the Honeymoon Rooms at the New York Plaza and he'd played bongos with James Dean in the Alexandria Suite of the Bel Air Hilton. But this was something else. The smell of teak and jasmine intoxicated him. No wonder Sinatra stayed here whenever he was in town. He followed the woman with the beehive through the main lounge. A colour TV flickered in a distant corner but the sound was turned down. As he passed the Chippendale dining table Martinez noticed some books. He stopped and picked them up. Rilke, Rimbaud and Baudelaire. There was also a copy of Allen Ginsberg's latest album *Sing Swing with Al*. It had been recorded live with the Nelson Riddle Orchestra at the Sands Hotel in Las Vegas.

"Good record," said the woman, "have you heard it?"

"No," said Martinez, "but I read the review in *Rolling Stone*. It said it was his best album since *Howl*."

"Oh, it's much better than *Howl*. His singing was terrible on that."

"Guess so," said Martinez, "but his trumpet playing's great."

They entered the second lounge which was just as big as the first.

"Is this your first time in London Mr Martinez?"

"I did a piece on Dino here two years ago. He was staying at the Ritz."

"Nice hotel," said the woman, "but we always insist on the Dorchester. It's a drain on the expense account but the Churchill is worth it for the security."

There was no denying that. When he'd stepped out of the cab on his arrival Martinez had been forced to push his way through a crowd of screaming girls all with their tearful eyes trained on the distant windows of the Churchill Suite up on the top floors. With the aid of a cop he'd eventually made it through the front doors but he'd had to shout to make himself heard at the reception desk.

They walked along a corridor lined with nineteenth century French miniatures until they came to another set of double-doors. The woman stopped.

"I'd better go in and check," she said. "You can never predict the artistic temperament."

Martinez nodded as she opened one of the doors and slipped in.

Was she kidding? He knew the artistic temperament alright. This was the guy Jean Harlow had attacked with an antique vase. He'd been soaked in Pina Colada by Jane Russell and, on one memorable occasion at the Excelsior Club in Hollywood, Mickey Rooney took exception to an off-the-cuff question about his latest divorce and, stretching up to his full height, he'd punched Martinez in the gut.

But it was all in the game. You didn't make it as the top showbiz writer in America without upsetting a few people.

"Ed baby! Great to see you! Come on in!"

It was Vern Golding, founder and Chairman of Golding Enterprises and the single most powerful figure in artist management. He wrapped a sweaty arm around Martinez's neck.

"Bet'cha didn't expect to see me eh big fella?"

He could say that again! Nobody ever knew what to expect from Vern Golding. Nicky Bernetti hadn't expected to be thrown through the window of his second floor apartment. Joe Somola hadn't expected to renegotiate his contract whilst sucking the barrel of a pump-load shotgun. And that young starlet in Vegas had definitely never expected twins.

"Vern, you're looking great!"

He looked like a sack of shit. With his belly straining the buttons of his Cardin shirt and with sweat beads glinting on his forehead, Vern was a coronary waiting to happen.

"Never felt better."

Laughing like a marine he stuck a Havana the size of salami between his teeth.

"Come on," he said, "let me fix you a drink."

He led Martinez to the bar.

"Lose yourself honey."

The woman in the beehive stopped in her tracks.

"But I –"

"But nothing sweetheart. You heard me. Scoot."

She opened her mouth to protest but then thought better of it. Shooting Martinez an uncomfortable and embarrassed look she turned swiftly on her stilettos.

"What'll it be Ed? The usual?"

"Yeah," said Martinez, trying to conceal his confusion, "why not?"

Golding laughed again, wheezing as if he'd swallowed a squeeze-box. Martinez sat on a bar stool and lit a Camel. He was eager to see what his "usual" actually was. Golding was searching through the bottles.

"Hey, I think we're in luck!"

He turned to Martinez and held up two bottles. Vodka and Chartreuse. Martinez smiled.

"Green Bitch," he said.

"Just like in Miami."

"You remembered that?"

"How the hell could I forget?" said Golding, "you must be the only son of a bitch in the world who actually drinks this shit!"

Green Bitch. This guy sure had a good memory.

It had been the *Misfits* launch in '62. Two hundred journalists flown in from all over America to the Wilson Presidential Hotel in Miami Beach. Luxury suites, special screenings, it had been one of Martinez's first cover stories. Everyone had wanted Monroe of course but the word was she'd high-tailed it to Acapulco in a fit of pique. Pissed, sweaty and Bedouin-thirsty, Martinez had slapped his notebook on the bar and ordered a Bud. He got talking to some guy from *Variety* who said the movie was a hill of shit in any case. Think about it, he said, they've gotta be desperate to set up this fucking circus. Monroe's nuthin but dinosaur meat and they know it. Here kid, take a look at this. He opened his briefcase and took out a glossy eight-by-twelve. Her name's Bardot and she's gonna be fuckin' dynamite, believe me. She's gonna blow Norma Jean clean outta the fuckin' water.

So why wasn't she in *Variety*?

The guy shifted in his seat and downed his scotch in one. Because she ain't Hollywood, he said bitterly, that's fuckin' why, and it ain't worth my while to go against the grain and to bite the hand that feeds me, you get my drift? Those guys can lean on you if you don't write pretty. You ever been to Hollywood kid? Martinez nodded but the guy from *Variety* looked at him with disdain. Yeah, he said, sure you have. Here, help me down.

Martinez took the guy's weight as he stepped off the bar-stool. Surprised at how drunk this guy actually was Martinez offered to help him with his jacket but the guy snatched it off him and became suddenly angry. You don't know shit college boy. You write fancy but you don't...know...shit. The last three words had been punctuated by three sharp prods to Martinez's stomach. These were followed by a semi-affectionate slap on the cheek and the stuffing of a ten dollar bill into his top pocket. Have a Gator on me pal.

Martinez watched as the guy turned around and walked out of the bar as if his briefcase weighed a ton. That's one drunk guy, said the bartender. Martinez nodded and hopped up onto the barstool again. He studied the eight-by-twelve of Bardot and opened his notebook.

Another Bud sir? It was the bartender again.

At first Martinez said yes but then he remembered the ten dollar bill the stranger had given him. He asked the bartender what a Gator was. The bartender laughed. Well sir, you could say it was something of a local speciality. Two parts vodka, one part Chartreuse, twist of lime, on the rocks. Martinez said he'd try one and the bartender smiled. Coming right up sir.

Licking the tip of his pencil, Martinez drew a sharp line through his embryonic notes for the Monroe article and turned to a new page. "The days of the great Hollywood studios are numbered," he wrote, "the tinsel castle with its celluloid kings and queens is about to be stormed and conquered by a new kind of star. The Golden Age is dead and the future belongs to Europe. The future belongs to Bardot."

In the margin he wrote a note reminding himself to get in touch with the Paris office as soon as he got back to New York. Perhaps Lecompte could set up an interview with Bardot? Martinez didn't think he'd have too much difficulty persuading the Showbiz Editor to go with the story. Just by looking at the photo it was clear that this Bardot kid was going to be huge and, with *Variety* tied up in a trunk with its vested interests in Hollywood, *Time*, for once, could get in there first.

Martinez smiled to himself as he tore out the page from his notebook and tucked it into his wallet. He placed the wallet in his jacket pocket and reached for the Gator which the bartender had just placed in front of him. The taste took him by surprise. He'd expected the reassuring warmth of the vodka but, instead, his mouth became bitter, sour and as dry as a ranch-hand's hat. The bartender started to laugh. You get used to it sir.

And he was right.

By nine o'clock the bar was full and Martinez was on his fourth Gator. His head swam pleasantly as, beside him, Hal Cruz from the *Los Angeles Tribune* and Marshall Fold from *Hollywood Star Monthly* argued over whether Monroe had really gone and flown down to Acapulco or not. They tried to get Martinez in on the discussion but Martinez didn't care about Monroe anymore. He sipped the Gator and thought about the blockbuster piece which would spring from the seeds in his wallet.

Hey, Martinez, you okay?

He told Cruz he was fine.

Well you don't look too good.

Martinez insisted that he'd never felt better.

There was a tense silence as Cruz studied Martinez's face as if he knew that he was holding something back but, before he had a chance to check it out, Fold stepped in and prodded Cruz in the chest.

Okay Mister Wise Guy, if Monroe ain't showing, how come Vern Golding's here?

With Cruz distracted, Martinez downed the Gator and ordered another. As he was fixing it the bartender turned around.

You know how the Gator got its name sir?

Martinez thought about it. He liked these kinds of games. He watched as the bartender unscrewed the Chartreuse and he suggested that maybe it was something to do with the colour? The bartender smiled.

No sir.

He poured the green liquid over the crackling ice cubes and added two shots of vodka before placing it on the bar.

It's called the Gator because – he leant in close – just when you think everything is calm – he came closer – and everything is real peaceful –

Martinez could now feel the heat of the bartender's breath on his chin and, with his interest aroused and with his concentration sharpened, he almost believed he could hear it. Suddenly the bartender brought his fist down to the bar with a bang. That's when it gets you!

Martinez was taken aback.

And you never see it coming.

The bartender laughed and Martinez suddenly found it annoying. He picked up his drink and turned back to face Cruz and Fold.

They were still discussing Monroe. Fold was getting red in the face. I tell you man, if Golding's here you just know something's gonna happen. Golding's got more fucking stars than Uncle Sam and he's got the studios by the balls so when you see him drag his big fat ass to Miami you just know that something's up!

Martinez couldn't focus. He'd only taken two small sips of his Gator but suddenly the room was spinning and the bartender's laughter sounded like it was coming from a public address system at a ball game. Fold's stare was like a judo hold.

C'mon Martinez, back me up here willya? Tell this dumb fuck!

Martinez felt a swelling in his stomach which sent a shiver up his spine and into his brain. All the sweat on his body froze and his tongue felt like someone else's. He heard Cruz telling Fold to keep his voice down.

What's eating you Cruz? Eh? Ever since I mentioned Golding's name you've been jumpy as hell! Is there something you ain't telling us? Are you on the fat bastard's payroll too?

Martinez took off his jacket and allowed it to drop to the floor. He reached for the Gator but he knocked it over and the glass rolled across the bar. The laughing bartender caught it just before it reached the edge. Martinez tried to smile but all he could do was leer.

C'mon Cruz, cut the bullshit. Has Golding bought you out too? Is that what's happened here? Is that why you're looking so shit-faced scared?

Cruz gave a sigh of resignation and Marshall Fold sensed triumph. He turned to the swaying Martinez.

You see Martinez? I knew it! I knew I'd get to the truth in the end!

He jumped up and down like a child but then Cruz calmed him down by putting his hand on his shoulder.

Fold, if you want to know the truth, he's standing right behind you.

Marshall Fold turned around slowly and came face to face with the powerful smile of Vern Golding.

Good evening gentlemen.

It was then that Martinez hopped off his stool and threw up all over Golding's freshly-pressed chinos.

"That's when you said 'Green Bitch!'"

"Yeah," said Martinez, "that bartender was right."

Golding laughed like a truck driver and slapped the journalist on the back but Martinez coiled up with embarrassment as he re-lived the time he'd vomited over one of the most influential men in Hollywood – a man who was now toasting his health a mere five yards away. Such forgiveness and magnanimity, qualities which one would never ordinarily associate with Vern Golding, made Martinez feel ashamed. He shifted uneasily on his barstool.

"Look," he said, "is it too late to say I'm sorry? I acted like a goddam fool that night."

Golding made a what-the-hell farting noise.

"Never waste your time on the past Martinez. I never did. Forget the past. The past is dead. In our business the future is all that counts."

"That's a sweeping philosophy."

"Don't knock it kid. It's a philosophy that's made me rich. And you wanna hear the funny part?"

Martinez nodded.

"I stole it from you."

"From me?"

"Sure. You remember this?"

From behind a cushion on one of the settees Golding picked up a July 1962 edition of *Time* and held it up for Martinez to see. On the cover was a picture of Brigitte Bardot in a swimsuit and beneath it, in huge letters, was the line "Bardot: The Shape of Things to Come by Ed Martinez". The author of the piece looked down rather sadly into his Gator.

"My first cover story," he said.

"That's right," said Golding excitedly, "all the other schmucks left Miami with their notebooks stuffed with half-baked no-stories about the Monroe no-show, but you," Golding waved the copy of *Time* in the air, "you were smart. You were one step ahead. You had your eyes on the future."

Martinez rolled the Gator gently.

"Yeah, but I got it wrong."

"Wrong? What are you talking about?"

Martinez looked up and related the story in a weary told-it-a-hundred-times-before tone.

"It was a piece about the Death of Hollywood but it never happened. By the time I made it to Paris, Bardot had already signed a six-picture deal with MGM. This had been arranged through a world-wide management buyout which had been negotiated by some guy who'd never even seen her movies. The machine swallowed her up and everything stayed the same. She made three pictures, a million bucks, then she freaked out and caught the first plane back to gay Paris. She claimed the States were corrupt. Her manager sued for breach of contract but he settled for an undisclosed figure which was enough to buy him three small islands in the Pacific."

There was a short silence before Golding pursed his lips and gave Martinez a respectful nod.

"I'm impressed with the detail," he said.

"I'm smart. You said so yourself."

Martinez raised his glass in a sardonic toast and took his first mouthful of Gator for four years. He winced and replaced it on the bar.

"Yeah," said Golding, "you're a smart kid. But you never figured out who that manager was."

"No, but I get this feeling you're gonna tell me."

Golding smiled. Tapped his chest.

"It was me."

Martinez tried hard not to look surprised but Golding saw straight through him.

"I know," he said, enjoying his little confession, "you're wondering how I got to hear of this Bardot kid when you thought she was all yours."

There was no denying it. Martinez had never known how Hollywood had managed to bag Bardot in the short space between his discovery of her and the publication of his article. He looked at Golding with a mixture of hatred and grudging respect before asking him the question he'd been dying to ask for years.

"How did you find her?"

"Easy," said Golding, "I just looked in your wallet."

Martinez jolted.

"My wallet?"

"Sure."

"But –"

"Oh come on, work it out Martinez. A guy gets wasted and he runs out of the bar after making a prime asshole of himself. He wakes up the following morning with his head buzzing like neon and he realizes something's missing."

It took a couple of seconds but when the truth finally hit Martinez it dropped to the pit of his stomach like a solid silver baseball.

"My jacket," he said.

Golding stretched out his arms to signal the end of the mystery. Martinez shook his head and rested it against the palm of his hand.

"Hey, don't be too hard on yourself Martinez. We both got something out of this. You got yourself a cover story and a name. I got a sulky French broad and three desert islands."

"I thought it was the bell-hop," said Martinez, his head still in his hands, "he came up in the morning and returned the jacket. He said he found it in the bar."

"That's what I told him to say."

Martinez looked up.

"I gave him ten bucks!"

Golding shrugged.

"Musta been his lucky day. I gave him fifty."

Martinez hopped off the barstool and ran his hand through his hair. He was trembling with a mixture of frustration and rage. He walked to the end of the bar. He walked back again. He looked at Golding and pointed the finger.

"You stole my jacket!"

"Are you kidding? I was the one who got it back to you!"

"But you looked inside my wallet!"

"Sure! How else was I going to know whose jacket I'd found?"

Martinez was stumped.

"Look," said Golding, coming up to Martinez and placing his arm on his shoulder, "after your buddies left I wiped myself down a little and got talking to some people and, just as I was sitting down at the bar to order a drink I noticed a jacket on the floor. It didn't seem to belong to anybody so I did what anybody else woulda done. I checked the pockets. I find the wallet and the first thing I see is a torn out piece of notepaper. Curiosity killed the cat Martinez. I open it up and what do I find but the Death of Hollywood and the coming of Brigitte Bardot. That's when I take out my notebook. I take down the name and I ring the office back in LA. 'Check out a Brigitte Bardot' I say, 'because *Time* reckon she's the future of cinema.' I make a note of your name too Martinez. I figure that when you ain't a drunken bum you're a man with his finger on the pulse. I put everything back in its place and I tell the bell-hop to take the jacket to you in the morning."

"But I was wrong," he said.

"About Bardot, yeah. But not about Hollywood."

"What do you mean?"

Golding leaned forwards and switched on the TV. It was a music show. Some bald guy with horn-rimmed glasses was playing clarinet with a band called The Philip Larkin Hot Four.

"Hollywood's dead, Martinez. I sold my interests six months ago."

Martinez shot him an incredulous stare.

"Don't look so shocked kid. I shoulda done it years ago. Hell, I shoulda done it when I read your goddam article!"

He unleashed another of his raucous laughs and slapped Martinez on the back. On the TV the bald guy with the horn-rimmed glasses approached the microphone and started to sing.

"That Whitsun I was late getting away..."

Golding took out a cigar from a box on the coffee table and lit it furiously with a solid-gold Zippo.

"I was still making money but there was no excitement. There was nothing new." He puffed out thick grey ribbons of smoke. "After it didn't work out with Bardot I got thinking about what you wrote. I went to New York and, one night, bored outta my stinking skull, I happened upon a bar in the Village and there it was. In the corner. The Future."

"Where sky and Lincolnshire and water meet..."

"It was just one guy with a guitar. He couldn't sing and his harp playing was shit but, and you'll appreciate this Martinez, the power was in the words. I couldn't even understand what the guy was saying half the time but I knew it was kinda special. Unique sounding, you know?"

Martinez nodded and Golding took it as a cue.

"Anyway, I asked this guy who the singer was and he looked at me as if I was crazy or something. 'Hey man,' he says, 'that's Dylan.' It didn't mean a fuck to me but I gave the bartender my card and told him to get this Dylan guy to give me a call."

"...and now and then a smell of grass..."

"Two days later he calls and we arrange to meet. He walks in like he's just got outta bed and I realize straight away I got problems. Like, this guy ain't no Cary Grant you know what I'm saying? He looks like a bum and I'm just about to suggest he go home and take a bath when he gives me this record. Turns out it's one of his. I put it on and it blows me away – no shit – so I ask him if he's got a manager. Yeah, he says, he's got ten of 'em, but none he can trust. Well I say 'trust me'. I had the contracts drawn and the rest is history. The guy's already a legend."

"Two US number ones," said Martinez.

"Yeah, and now a sell-out English tour."

Golding sat back and sucked contentedly on his cigar. Martinez watched the bald singer on TV as he drew back from the microphone at the end of the song and bowed to the receptive crackling audience.

"That Larkin guy sings good," said Martinez.

Golding gave a disparaging grimace.

"That kind of good-time shit is dead Martinez. The kids don't buy it anymore. Ginsberg, Sinatra and that Auden guy. The kids don't need no more wrinklies in tuxedos. They need something new. Something that's exciting. Look –"

He picked up a pile of long-playing records and flicked through them theatrically. "The US Top Five," he said, "*Auden Sings Isherwood*, *The Big Band Sound of Robert Frost*, *Tony Bennett's Greatest Hits*, *Sinatra Sings The Modernists* and *Ezra Pound and His Cajun Banjos*. It's the moms and dads Martinez. They're the ones buying this shit."

He threw the records across the floor and stood up.

"Where's the passion? Where's the energy and the guts? For a while there was Ginsberg sure – but he came outta the Army with his beard shaved off and now he sings schmaltzy duets on TV with Como."

Martinez was momentarily distracted by a loud and discordant sound which came from behind a door in the corner. It resonated for a few seconds before mutating violently into a high-pitched whine. Golding checked his watch and walked towards the mysterious door.

"I wanna get that excitement back Martinez. I want the danger and the guts. There's a whole generation out there that's aching to spend its dollars and dimes on something that's real. You and me Martinez, we're gonna give it to them!"

"Me?"

"Don't look so shocked kid. From that time in Miami I knew you were a guy with his eye on the future. When I set up this tour I had the press on the phone twenty-four hours a day but, all the while, I kept thinkin' about the guy who wrote the Bardot piece. Get Ed Martinez. I said. He's the only one who understands."

"But I don't understand!"

There was another loud burst of noise from behind the door. Golding gave a wry smile.

"You will when I tell you that, tonight, at the Royal Albert Hall, Dylan is going electric!"

He opened the door and the feedback spilled in.

"Hey Dylan," yelled Golding, "come out here. There's someone I want you to meet!"

Martinez stood up in expectation. He'd heard all the protest songs and he'd seen Dylan play from the back of a cotton truck on *Hootenanny*.

"Here's my boy!"

Golding threw a fatherly arm around Dylan's shoulder and punched him playfully in the shoulder.

"This is Ed Martinez. The best fucking journalist in America!"

Martinez couldn't believe it. Dylan had gone through a transformation. The clean-cut guy with the short hair and checked shirt had turned into some kind of leather monster. He'd lost a lot of weight too. His waist was only slightly thicker than the neck of the Fender Stratocaster he was holding in his hand. The face was inscrutable because of the dark glasses and his hair was longer, shaggier – and far redder than Martinez had imagined.

"Let's have a drink," said Golding, reaching for a bottle of champagne from the cooler and popping it open, "let's toast our success!"

Dylan just flopped into a chair like a hobo.

"After all," said Golding, froth cascading over his hands, "we've just sold eighteen thousand double albums in just one day. I think it's a record!"

He went to the bar and took out three glasses.

"And tonight is when we change everything!"

He licked the back of his hand and poured out two glasses. He gave the first to Martinez and offered the second to Dylan but Dylan just shook his head.

"C'mon," said Golding, "loosen up!"

Dylan shot him a cold Ray-Ban stare. Golding sighed.

"Shall I fix you a beer or something? Whaddya want Dylan?"

"Bugger all."

Martinez sat down on the settee and sipped his champagne tentatively. Golding, clearly deflated slightly but determined not to show it, lifted his glass.

"The future!"

"The future," said Martinez.

Golding downed his glass in one and belched like a hog.

Dylan ruffled his hair and yawned. He picked up the phone and Martinez listened as that unmistakeable Welsh accent ordered room service to bring up some more laver bread.

III

A DIGRESSION REGARDING THE DANGERS OF EXCESSIVE HOSPITALITY

(AND THE LEGENDARY UNPREDICTABILITY OF THE WASP)

THE NOBLE and esteemed Salaam-el-Duur (eloquent and vivid demographer of the Arabian peninsulas) describes in the fifth volume of his Histories of Persia how the Portuguese explorer Diogo Alvares suffered unpropitious predicaments whilst negotiating the trackless oven of the Kalahambara desert. Indeed, his series of misfortunes persisted when he and his caravan momentarily escaped the endless furnace and chanced upon the perceived sanctuary of Wadi-Washm. This mountain-side settlement (carved into the yielding rock until, over the centuries, it had achieved the wondrous complexity and intricacy of a subterranean municipality on a par with any provincial conurbation in England) had once hosted a thriving community of Tuerian citizens. The Tuerians, by Salaam's accounts, were a singularly sophisticated and ingenious tribe who had succeeded in harnessing the power of a most fearsome creature for their continued sustenance – namely the Kalahambara Wasp.

This particular insect had exceeded all previously-known laws of entomological proportions and had achieved dimensions broadly commensurate with our elusive and lovable fellow, the common wren. However, his enormity was complemented by a suitably capacious brain. Salaam recounts how this wasp would organize itself into regimented squadrons which descended on the multifarious enemies of the tribe in times of threat almost as if the settlement of Wadi-Washm was their own! In return for these charitable strategic campaigns against the advances of rapacious desert wolves and rodents, the wasp was rewarded with bowls of sweet goat's milk. Tragically, the cool and ambrosial elixir of the goat's milk gradually produced a calamitous transformation on the previously benevolent Kalahambara Wasp. Within weeks of ingesting copious quantities of this libation the nubile insect experienced a hideous metamorphosis from willing ally and defender of the fold to a vehement devil! Naturally, the response of the confused citizens of Wadi-Washm in encountering such a vicious and hitherto unrepresentative element of life's tribulations was to flee their mountain haven and unanimously rush into the unforgiving terrain of the mighty Kalahambara – and into the arms of the Grim Reaper!

Their unfortunate bones were a full fathom beneath the shifting desert waves by the time Diogo Alvares and the ragged remnants of his company chanced upon the ruins of Wadi-Washm. Feverish with excitement at a momentary respite from their usual tenure in precarious marquees with walls of ripped canvas, the men gathered their rags and climbed the stairways to the coolness of the dark, carved cottages up above. Deaf to the warnings of their captain regarding the twin-pronged stab of the fat-tailed desert scorpion (a most unsociable fellow who thrived in such murky domiciles), the men promptly succumbed to the narcotic spells of Orpheus.

Salaam-el-Duur recounts how Diogo was the first to be tripped from his weary slumbers by a reverberation which appeared to originate in the very core of the Earth itself. Alarmed to discover granules of sand dispersing around his hands as if they were dancing on the surface of a constantly-beaten drum, the stout-hearted pilgrim jumped to his feet, unsheathed his sword and scanned the skies in full anticipation of meeting his doom at the claws of some previously un-encountered and fearsome desert ogre! But this fine warrior detected another sound within the Satanic rumbling – a sound so shrill and acute it forced him to drop his weapon and cover his ears for fear of being delivered to the very gates of delirium! It was then that Diogo Alvares witnessed a Stygian cloud of swirling smoke approaching him at the speed of a galloping Alentejo mare – mercilessly engulfing the ground like a d---able tornado! The mystery of the discordant cacophony was revealed to him as being the screams of his hapless men as they attempted, in vain, to outrun it! Diogo watched with despair as his crew were consumed in this nefarious vortex. It must have become quickly evident to him that this was no Earthly cyclone at all!

Regarding the origin of this malignant hurricane I would beseech your indulgence for but a few moments as I direct your attention to the its source – namely the dank interiors of the lofty Wadi-Washm lodges. Here, long expurgated of the tragic human tenants, that Machiavellian fiend, the Kalahambara Wasp had colonized these hidden corners with characteristic assiduity – constructing vast nests which pulsated nightly with the energy of a Lancashire cotton mill. This impressive gnat had a most capacious intelligence and he possessed a vivid recollection of the somnific sweetness of the goat's milk which it had tasted in its infancy and now that mankind had returned to the hitherto deserted upper echelons of the Wadi-Washm in the form of Diogo Alvares's desert-weary band, the Kalahambara Wasp had assumed that where there was Man there was also the likelihood of goat's milk! Aroused into a frenzy by the anticipation of tasting once again this lacteal ambrosia, the winged devils had spilled from their barracks and instigated a nocturnal campaign against Diogo's exhausted party.

Diogo's surprising source of salvation was none other than the decayed corpse of a one-humped dromedary which lay nearby and whose muscle, crucial organs and bowels had been ripped out by ravenous packs of desert hounds. And thus it was that the rapidly debilitating figure of Diogo Alvares crawled along the ribbed and unforgiving trail of the Kalahambara desert within the protective shell of the increasingly pungent dromedary, propelled slowly – but effectively – by means of apertures he'd sliced in the bottom of the hide with his dagger. But the ireful cloud of hornets had persisted in following him from the Wadi-Washm and they besieged him – rapping the walls of his asylum like freshly-dispatched musket shells! But Fate must have been in good humour that day for Diogo Paredus do Carmo Alvares was rescued, and awoke within the walls of that last surviving secret wonder of the ancient world, Carthon!

On awakening from his involuntary period of dormancy, Diogo Alvares must have indicated to him that he had indeed slipped free of Earth's mortal bondage and entered the sublime pastures of Paradise! For were not the sheets which enveloped his enfeebled form woven of the finest silk? Were not the tables which surrounded his monumental bed overflowing with all manner of nuts, fruits and gelatinous confections? Salaam informs us that Diogo struggled to depart the wondrous haven of his berth for this most commodious sanctum was as soft as a meadow in early summer! As if to further enhance this pastoral illusion, the chamber housed hundreds of tame songbirds whose fluttering wings and chirruping cantatas filled the room.

When he eventually pulled back the silk sheets and approached the window, Diogo Alvares witnessed the full, irreproachable beauty of Carthon.

He was enchanted by the voluptuous white domes of the temples, the jubilant cornucopia of mosaics which embellished the mighty city walls, the spear-like turrets of the shimmering minarets and the maze of alleys and thoroughfares which wove a magical tapestry around the bustling bazaars, piazzas and palaces. But his admiring gaze was suddenly disturbed by the sound of the doors to his quarters being thrown open.

Enthusiasts of the Histories of Persia often cite the startling appearance of King Ramak-el-Beyerty as one of the most arresting passages in the entire opus! Salaam-el-Duur's quill delineates a most splendid figure sporting a large barruk turban (woven from the gossamer silk of the Ragano worm). His corpulent form was cloaked in abundant blue robes whose lengthy train was suspended from the delicate hands of twenty beautiful young women – each plucked carefully from the most elevated regions of the King's fruitful harem. So ethereal were these mademoiselles that we are told they skipped across the floor without emitting a sound rather as if nature had somehow reprieved them of the more burdensome aspects of palpable physicality!

King Ramak-el-Beyerty stepped into the middle of the room, unfurled a vellum scroll and began to declaim in imperfect Portuguese.

"Dear honoured guest, I, King Ramak-el-Beyerty – Ruler of all the Western Plains of the Kalahambara and Emperor of the Ridged Desert of Washm from the Rugut Oasis to the Palm Rings of Ammaraud – on behalf of all the proud burghers of Carthon do greet you and now extend to you our boundless hospitality. It is the proud custom and tradition of the city of Carthon to excel in the arts of hospitality. Our reputation for the provision of pleasure to our sadly infrequent guests is celebrated in verse by all the finest poets from the Jebel scrublands of the north down to the desolate southern slopes of Adrar."

The King clapped his hands once more and the doors at the far end of the chamber opened to reveal a procession of servants holding aloft golden banqueting trays heavy with the ambrosial cargo of Carthon's masterly culinarians. Cuts of mutton garnished with fragrant sprigs of rosemary and mint! Thin strips of roasted fowl basted with apricots and olmehra leaves! Lamb kio-babs with peppers and fenugreek seeds on a steaming mound of fragrant rice! Sheep's milk sweetened with wild vanilla!

The legendary hospitality of Carthon did not abate and over the following days and weeks Diogo Alvares was awoken with a feast worthy of Demeter herself! Once satiated, the empty salvers would be returned to the kitchens and twenty further jewels from the royal harem were ushered in, quickly lavishing upon Diogo the fruits of their specialized apprenticeship. This feast of various delights was visited upon Diogo thrice daily and such was the plentiful reserves and variety of Carthon's famous hospitality that not one dish, nor one maiden, was ever visited upon him a second time!

But Diogo Alvares was fired by peril and uncertainty – not lust or gluttony – and so this legendary city soon became a wearisome, cushioned prison of frippery and carnal indulgence! Witnessing his rapidly accumulating corpulence, he cursed the pertinacious attentions of Carthon's cooks! Indeed, his body had now bulged so dramatically that his ragged apparel – stretched to the limits of their durability like well-worn sails had finally surrendered to the inevitable and disintegrated!

Finally, after twelve full months had elapsed (and with his bed long-since collapsed from the burden of his obesity) Diogo arose after yet another gargantuan breakfast and, using all that remained of his dissipated strength, he clambered like an unsteady giant towards the arched window of his chamber. He peered down into the square of the bazaar down below and calculated that the distance between the ledge of his cell and the sanctuary of the ground was but roughly equivalent to the height of a mizzen-mast. Naturally, having negotiated similar heights many times previously during his adventures Diogo Alvares concluded that here was a most felicitous means of escape from his peculiar confinement! But whilst it was doubtlessly true that, ordinarily, Diogo Alvares would have succeeded in negotiating a leap of twenty feet with no critical impediment to his flight, the addled buccaneer had overlooked the painful particulars of his present condition. For Diogo, in his eagerness to abscond, had committed a calamitous miscalculation! For whereas in his imagination the Portuguese explorer persisted in envisaging himself as the agile and lean athlete who had swung so effortlessly from the masts of the Santo Antonio, in truth he was now a huge figure and this disparity between the concrete and the fanciful formed the crucial basis for this mission's failure!

For three long days and three equally interminable nights, fifty of King Ramak-el-Beyerty's finest warriors pulled hard on the ropes that had been tied around Diogo's inflated form in an effort to release him from his predicament of being trapped in the window of his chamber. In addition to these efforts, fifty burly cavalrymen of His Majesty's camel troop were subsequently instructed to augment this desperate action by occupying the interior of the chamber and pushing Diogo from the rear in the hope that it would dislodge his stricken bulk. Despite these Herculean endeavours however, Diogo Alvares remained cemented in the window – his face transformed into a deep shade of heliotrope by the malevolent furnace of the sun.

But King Ramak-el-Beyerty was a most resourceful and astute potentate and, realizing that inordinate measures were called for if a terrible conclusion was to be avoided, he raised the ceremonial trimpitta to his lips and produced a shrill alarum.

Ah reader, what a most singular spectacle followed this call! The very ground shook and trembled as the combined forces of the King's elephant guards thundered forth on their magnificent steeds! Twelve immaculately-attired Carthonite sat astride each beast, each clinging on to a sturdy leash woven from the sinewy fronds of bohamash grass. Slipping down from their elevated positions with liquid grace, the riders looped thick ropes around the elephants' flailing trunks and – after striking their steeds' leathery hides with their ebony katrams – the obedient creatures responded by heaving with all their considerable might until the network of ropes tightened and sang! King Ramak-el-Beyerty was overjoyed for, in a mere matter of minutes, he could see that Diogo's body was loosened from the painful grip of the window!

But, oh, how fickle the whims of fortune! How instantaneous the transformation from joy to despondency!

Reader, the breathtaking depth and capacious dimensions of the crater which was formed in the central square following Diogo Alvares's forced descent is said to have rivalled that of the infamous basin in the southernmost regions of the Kalahambara desert After the mighty clouds of dust had finally dissipated, King Ramak-el-Beyerty and his assembled subjects tentatively gathered around the edge and peered into the abyss in astonished silence. The unhappy sight that greeted them was that of Diogo Alvares's lifeless body splayed out in all its naked indignity upon four crushed elephants.

King Ramak-el-Beyerty's grief at his guest's undignified demise was most profound and it was peculiarly undiminished by the passage of time. Thirty years later – when this most sagacious monarch himself succumbed to the Reaper's callous scythe (after innocently upturning a stone and encountering the wrathful ire of a green-ribbed scorpion) – his advisors discovered that he had long-since expressed in his private papers the heartfelt desire to be interred after his death alongside Diogo Alvares in the self-same tomb on the Washm tundra.

Four hundred loyal Carthonites followed the train of camels which transported his body through the city gates and out across the desert but only three hundred and fifty of them succeeded in completing the journey back. The remainder lay strewn around the tomb, their faces frozen in expressions of abject terror.

Their ravaged carcasses a seething mass of wasps.

IV

THEME PARK

1999. It was an invasion. Huge trucks and digging machines rumbled like tanks through the villages and men in hard hats filled up the local caffs. Fights broke out in The Flying Fox and protest groups lined the entrance of the Theme Park site to try and stop the lorries. My mum said it reminded her of the miner's strike.

Wales Today arrived. They filmed a pitched battle between the police and the hippies which later won some kind of award. There were fifty arrests and one policeman lost an eye. The place was in chaos. And then the phone rang.

"It's Ed."

I should have known.
"See it?"
"What?"
"The news."
"Oh yeah. Terrible isn't it?"
I hear him pull hard on a cigarette.
"Ed," I said, "maybe we should back off."
"No way!"
"But all these reports!"
"Meet me."
"Where?"
"The pub."
"When?"
"Now."

The phone clunked and purred. I replaced the receiver and ran a comb through my hair. I looked a mess but the dole did that to you. I only shaved on Giro day. That was the only time I could afford to go out.

Ed was halfway through a Guinness when I arrived. He'd bought me a Grolsch. I popped it open.
"It's sorted."
"What? Just like that?"
Ed smiled.
"Five weeks."
"A bit quick."
"It's business."

Ed and me had history. We'd gone to school together, we'd smoked dope together, we'd picked up girls together and we'd signed on together. In all that time I'd never heard him say a sentence that contained more than two words. Not that he was thick or anything. Far from it. He knew about the arts.

"What's *The Ancient Mariner* about?"

"A bird."

"*Under Milk Wood*?"

"A village."

"*Battleship Potemkin*?"

"A pram."

He was a punk conversationalist.

He was also shrewd. As a kid he'd once stored snowballs in his mum's freezer during the winter and then sold them for twenty pence each in July.

"So what did they say?"

Ed shrugged.

"It's coming."

"When?"

"August."

"And they want us to do it?"

He nodded.

"Even though we've got no experience?"

He shrugged again. He reached into his pocket and took out a wad of papers which had been stapled together. He flattened it out on the table and handed me a pen.

"Sign."

"What is it?"

"A contract."

"With who?"

"With them."

"What does it say?"

"Just sign."

"Can't I read it first?"

"What for?"

"In case they rip us off."

"They won't."

"How do you know?"

He smiled.

"Trust me."

It had all started with the camera. An uncle of mine had won a small fortune on the lottery and he came back to Wales to buy presents for his relatives. It was only the second time I'd ever met him and I felt a bit guilty as we stood in Dixon's waiting for my mum to decide how many tellies she wanted.

"And what would you like Dean?" He spread out his arms as if he was showing me Arizona. "Anything at all. My treat. Don't be shy."

He had an awful fixed smile and I suddenly realized that this guy was feeling more guilty than me.

Guilty for having never written to my mother.

Guilty for having not returned for his father's funeral.

Guilty because he was rich.

And guilty because he's just remembered my name wasn't Dean.

"I'll have that."

I'd pointed at over five grand's worth of video equipment.

"Wrap it up," said my uncle.

"Right away sir," said the salesman.

Six weeks passed. They video equipment stayed in its boxes. They were piled up in the corner of my bedroom and covered with a sheet. One day, skint and in between Giros, I invited Ed round to see how much he reckoned I could get for it all in Muddy Taylor's Second Hand Shop. Ed sat on the edge of the bed and snapped a can of Heineken. I unveiled the boxes like a cheap magician and, when I turned around, Ed's face was white. His mouth had dropped open and Heineken froth was dripping down his arm.

"Ed, are you okay?"

He looked at me as if I'd just shown him a headless corpse. Then he gave a stunned little nod. He came over for a closer look.

"I could put it in *The Leader*," I said, "but I haven't got the readies. Do you think Muddy's give me five hundred?"

"Five hundred?"

"Well, four then."

"You're mad!"

"Well how much then? You tell me!"

"For this?"

"Yeah."

"All in?"

"Yeah."

"Jesus Christ!"

He turned away and faced the window. He took a sip of Heineken and I noticed that his hands were shaking.

"Ed, I –"

"Shut up."

"What?"

"I'm thinking."

I left him to it. That was the best way with Ed. Whatever he had to say he'd get round to it in the end. I went downstairs to make a pot of tea. The kettle was just about to boil when Ed thundered down the stairs. He entered the kitchen with an excited look on his face.

"Pink Rat," he said.

Pink Rat used to be the school band but now they signed on like everyone else. Ed's plan was to do a promo for them and get it on to MTV. He'd always been obsessed with television and now, with my gear, he reckoned he'd discovered his ticket out of the valleys.

We hired the hall of the old Miner's Institute for an afternoon and devoted three hours of tape to Pink Rat performing a song called 'Nuke the Vatican'. When we finished I needed a drink. Pink Rat said they'd buy us one.

The Flying Fox was full. Workmen from the Theme Park site crowded the lounge and there was a row of hard hats and mobiles all along the bar. We went into the snug and sat next to a couple of hippies who were feeding crisps to a dog. When *Wales Today* came on we all looked up at the telly. Once again the scenes at the Theme Park site dominated everything. The reports showed workmen being driven into the park in buses. They were pelted with stones from the demonstrators and, when the cops moved in, there was a big fight. The reporter was jostled and the picture got jerky. Someone held a hand up towards the lens and then there was a sharp edit. They returned to the studio and we returned to our beers.

"I went to a Theme Park once," This was Del, the bass player. "In Germany it was. They had a bungee jump. Me and my sister did it. You jumped off this crane like. It was brilliant. I've got it on tape."

A funny look came over Ed's face. His earlier despondency at the realization that Pink Rat were never going to make it on to MTV was suddenly swept away.

"On tape?"

"Yeah. VHS. They record your jump and sell it to you afterwards."

"They're getting one here," said the singer. "I saw it in *The Leader*. BUNGEE JUMP SET FOR THEME PARK it said. Some guys from Canada or something. It said they were millionaires."

"This tape," said Ed.

Del's face lit up.

"Would you like to see it?"

"Yes."

"Okay. When?"

"Right now."

From the moment he saw the rather blurry record of Del's bungee jump, Ed was a man with a mission. He persuaded me to set up a meeting with

Kevin Spray, the Amenities Manager at the new Theme Park site. Ed reckoned that, with our video equipment, we could approach the owners of the Canadian bungee jump with a business proposal. They provide the jump, we tape it, it didn't sound very convincing to me but the Amenities Manager seemed to like it because a certain amount of the business proposals had to be ring-fenced to favour local enterprises and this seemed to fit the bill perfectly. He said he'd follow it up and then we shook hands. Once outside Ed punched the sky and shouted 'yes!' It was the first thing he'd said all afternoon. Now, a month later, here I was fiddling with the top of a Grolsch bottle in the snug of The Flying Fox.

"Just sign." Said Ed.

"Hang on."

The stapled pad of contracts and waiver forms had been faxed to Kevin Spray's office that afternoon. A courier had then delivered them to Ed's mum's house and Ed, eager to get going, had signed them immediately. I flicked through some of the pages. The Buffalo Dive Bungee Crew from Ontario could obviously afford good lawyers. Some of the small print was the size of bacteria.

"What's wrong?"

"Nothing. I'm just reading it through."

Ed sighed wearily and drummed his fingers on the table. Then he stood up and went to the bar. I was relieved. It was impossible to think straight with him staring at me all the time.

"Want one?"

"No thanks. I'm fine."

I held up the half-full Grolsch as evidence and returned to the stapled pad. I still couldn't concentrate though. The events of the past month kept racing through my head like old-fashioned newsreel. I thought about the big gang of ex-miners who had joined the protest groups outside the Theme Park site gates. They were angry because they'd heard about a proposed new ride called 'The Big Shaft'. This was a Virtual Reality trip through the catacombs of a coalmine at high speed. A company from Japan had been busy for weeks putting the final touches to it. The ex-miners had pointed out that The Miner's Heritage Centre, which was only five miles away (and on which many of the men relied upon for their livelihoods) already had a Virtual Reality coalmine ride. They admitted that it wasn't exactly 'state of the art' but it was their most popular attraction and it brought in the crowds. 'The Big Shaft' represented unfair competition in their eyes and the Centre might now face closure.

"Nonsense," said a man from the Tourist Board on *Wales Today*. "There is no reason why the Miner's Heritage Centre and the new Theme Park should not co-exist."

Later in the same programme they dropped an item and returned live to the Theme Park gates. Yushami Wakamoto, the Director of Anatagata Virtual Reality (Japan) Ltd., had turned up unexpectedly and the place had erupted into violence. Ex-miners had broken through the security barriers and police with riot shields had been rushed in from Cardiff but they were too late to save Mr Wakamoto. He'd been taken to Merthyr General with suspected skull fracture. Apparently an ex-miner had whacked him over the head with a lump of coal.

That's when ITN got interested.

A crew was sent down from London and they checked into the Guest House owned by Ed's mum. Dazzled by their gear and their sexy lifestyles, Ed hadn't been slow to make friends (although the Londoners were still slightly bemused by his unorthodox approach to conversation). He helped them load their gear every morning and, in return, Nick Hodges, the cameraman, had promised to show Ed a few tricks of the trade after they'd finished covering the protests. From that moment, Bruce Willis had been deposed as Ed's all-time hero and his vocabulary had been enriched by a new word.

Nick.

"There's Nick!"

I looked up from the stapled pad. Nick Hodges and his sound guy had just walked in. Ed wiped a blob of Guinness foam from his upper lip.

"Hey Nick!"

Nick raised his arm in acknowledgement and he came over to join us. The sound guy followed with two lagers.

"Where's Julian?" asked Ed. Julian was the reporter.

"Talking to his missus on the mobile," said the sound guy.

Nick raised his pint to his lips and adopted a conspiratorial tone.

"Problems at home."

"Always happens," said the sound guy. "If he's away for more than two days Nicole's on the blower furious as fuck. You'd think she'd understand by now."

"Remember Sarajevo?"

"Shit," said the sound guy. "How could I forget?"

"That was the worst."

"By far. It was tragic."

"What happened?" asked Ed. He was like an eager puppy.

Nick and the sound guy looked at each other. They were wondering whether to tell the story or not. In the end the sound guy gave a what-the-hell shrug.

"We saw this old bloke," he said, "must have been at least seventy but he was dashing about like a teenager."

"He was carrying a bucket," said Nick, "heading for the water pump."

The sound guy shook his head solemnly.

"Nobody does that."

"Not in daylight."

"Not in Sarajevo."

"Anyway," said Nick, "I switched to record and we followed him. Julian came too. We reached the square and the old bloke stopped. The pump was on the other side. To reach it he'd have to run across thirty yards of exposed ground."

"We knew he'd never make it," said the sound guy.

"Those snipers were shit hot," said Nick. "They could clip the balls off a bluebottle."

The sound guy leant forward.

"I had all the levels ready," he said. "Gunshots can really fuck them up if you're not careful."

Nick took over.

"So the old bloke takes a deep breath and goes for it. He's halfway across, still swinging his stupid bucket when..."

He looked away in sadness and disgust. He picked up his lager and sipped it slowly. Ed was on tenterhooks. He turned to the sound guy.

"When what?"

The sound guy looked at Nick and sighed heavily.

"Julian's fucking mobile went."

"I had him as well," said Nick, desperately trying to contain his anger. "Right in the middle of frame. The bullet gets grandad in the hip and he goes sprawling. It was a beautiful shot. I even had the upturned bucket in focus but, just as the slug is fired, what do I hear? Loud as a fucking bell? 'Nicole, not now sweetheart. I'm really busy!' Jesus Fucking Christ!"

"Shouldn't have called him at work," said the sound guy.

"That would have been a BAFTA winner," said Nick, "no doubt about it. Instead Phil Wheen from the Beeb got it for some shit about Rwanda. Anyone could do that. Starving kids are easy. All you've got to do is lock off the camera and fill the fucking frame!"

"Julian was very apologetic," said the sound guy. "But it was too late. The call had spooked Nick and jolted the shot. By now the old bloke was bleeding like a pig and screaming his head off. ITN would never have cleared it. Too upsetting. We carried on recording for a bit. We reckoned that if the sniper tried to finish the job then we might be able to dub the second shot over the first one and lose Julian's voice but no such joy. An ambulance arrived and it fucked up all the levels."

He looked at Nick rather nervously.

"Fancy a scotch?"

Nick gave a serious little nod and the sound guy stood up.

"Would you lads like anything?"

I told him we were fine and he went off to the bar with a twenty pound note. Ed took the stapled pad from me with a smile. Stunned by the story, I'd signed it without thinking.

Three months passed. Mr Wakamoto recovered and went back to Japan wearing a turban. The protests dwindled and ITN lost interest. Nick and the crew were recalled to London.

In late April the Theme Park opened to the public and became an instant success. Queues formed at eight o'clock in the morning and, after a few weeks, permission was granted by the council to build an overflow coach parking area. Tony Blair came and bought a candy floss. Two days later William Hague won an enormous panda on the Coconut Shy. The village was crowded again. Ed's mum drew up plans for an extension to the Guest House and Betty from The Flying Fox bought a Mercedes convertible on the proceeds of her steak and kidney pudding.

Me and Ed were doing well too.

In our first month we made enough to rent a large flat above the Rediffusion showroom. I signed off, got myself a credit card, opened a saver's account to prepare for the quiet winter months and I splashed out on an Armani suit from a posh shop in Cardiff. At first I'd been worried about signing a contract with the Canadians but, in practice, everything was cool.

The bungee ride cost thirty quid.

The video was ten.

Six of that was ours.

With anything up to three hundred punters a day me and Ed were making a fortune.

But Ed wasn't happy.

Filming hysterical Germans and Americans as they hurtled to an abrupt bounce just ten feet away from certain death wasn't good enough for him. The ITN crew had impressed him and he was now more desperate than ever to be a professional news cameraman. He applied for a trainee place with BBC Wales but he didn't even get an interview. I tried to tell him that you needed a degree to get into television but Ed wouldn't listen. He'd got the bug. He wanted to go to Bosnia with Kate Adie. He wanted to huddle in the back of a Land Rover filming one of John Simpson's pieces to camera.

One day I turned up at our video podium at the Theme Park to find Ed and the camera missing. There was a note on the table in our makeshift office. It said 'back soon'.

I had to fob off the punters all day with a lie about 'technical difficulties' but I didn't think I was very convincing.

Ed turned up later at The Flying Fox. Apparently there had been a major fire at a tyre warehouse in Barry and he'd gone there to film it hoping that *Wales Today* might use it as 'amateur footage'. They weren't interested. None of it got used.

The Canadians were furious. One more stunt like that, they said, and they'd sue us for breach of contract.

"Fuck them," said Ed.

We went back to the flat and watched Mad Max on our brand new Sony widescreen.

Ten days after the public opening there was an 'official' opening and all the Theme Park amenities staff received letters from Kevin Spray telling us to dress smartly because Prince Charles was turning up. I wore my Armani suit and stood next to Ed at the end of a long line as we waited our turn to shake hands with the Royal Party. The party consisted of Prince Charles, Prince William and Sheik Zair Al-Haddid.

The Sheik was sixteen and was Prince Williams's best friend at Eton. All through the late winter and early spring the tabloids had printed feature after feature about the new Royal Chum. There had been photos of his palace in Kuwait, his flat in Kensington, his silver-plated Bentley (which he could drive as soon as he passed his test) and the birthday cake in the shape of an oil-rig that he'd received from his father, Harif Al-Haddid, the twelfth richest man in the world. *The Sun* had even printed 'Ten Things You Never Knew about Our Willie's Little Pal'. The list included, at number six:

Zair Al-Haddid's full name is Zair Hannad Mustaf Best Charlton Law Muhammad Al-Haddid. His dad is a huge Man Utd fan.

The two friends were now following Prince Charles as Kevin Spray led him along the parade of amenities staff. At every fourth person or so the Prince would stop and have a brief chat. The routine was a well-practised one.

He'd laugh.

He'd look serious and ask a question.

He'd nod.

He'd crack the illusion of a private joke and then he'd walk off, tugging at his cuff links and half-turning to give the impression that he'd love a longer chat but time was against him.

Behind the ticker-tape line about twenty yards away the photographers clicked and whirred like a jungle. Some of them were standing on step-ladders and begging Prince William or the young Sheik to give them a smile.

Ed was furious. All morning he'd been hearing reports of a massive pile-up on the Severn Bridge. He wanted to sneak off and film the casualties with our new digi-cam but it was impossible to move. There were security guards and secret agents everywhere. He was forced to hang around the park all day in a suit two sizes too small.

"You're Ed."

"That's right."

Prince Charles stood right in front of him.

"Camera fellow."

"Him too."

"Your friend?"

"Yes sir."

"How much?"

"Ten quid."

"Not bad."

"Good value."

"Busy?"

"Heaving."

"Super."

You had to hand it to the Prince. He certainly did his research.

Three hours later, after all the press and the photographers had been shepherded away, me and Ed were sitting on a bench outside the hospitality tent when a bloke in *Reservoir Dogs* shades came over. He sat down and took out an ID card. It showed a picture of a bloke wearing shades.

"We need someone to stay behind for a bit tonight boys."

"Oh yeah?"

Ed was moody. He'd missed his chance to sell the pile-up to *Wales Today* and now he was drowning his sorrows with a scotch.

"The young Sheik wants a bungee jump," said the bloke. "He also wants a vid."

Ed swallowed the last of his scotch and crushed the plastic cup.

"Prince William wanted a go too," said the bloke, "but we couldn't allow it. He's having a right royal sulk at the moment."

The corner of his mouth curled up. It was probably his idea of a smile. He reached for something in the inside pocket of his jacket. Ed and I caught a glimpse of a shoulder holster and the butt of a pistol. We looked at each other. You obviously didn't mess with this bloke. What he took out was a brown envelope. He placed it on the table.

"Open it."

I opened it. Inside there was five hundred quid in cashpoint-crisp tenners.

"Yours," said the bloke. "I take it we're sorted?"

"Yeah," I said. "Sorted."

"Good. Come with me."

Our camera gear had been taken out of the night storage room and set up in its usual place on the podium. This was fifty yards away from the bungee crane.

"We took the liberty," said the bloke.

He took out his walkie-talkie and spoke to another bloke in shades who appeared out of a bush in the distance.

The whole place was empty.

No punters. No screams.

Nothing.

Then I looked to my left and saw Prince Charles. He was in shirtsleeves and wearing a pair of Raybans. Prince William followed, his head bowed and his hands in his pockets. He kicked a plastic cup that was lying about on the ground and Prince Charles told him off. Ed, noticing that the bloke in shades was still using the walkie-talkie, switched on the camera and started recording. He turned to me and winked. I began to feel uncomfortable.

Prince Charles and Prince William were joined by Kevin Spray, a local MP and a crop of other VIPs. There was no sign of the Sheik but, when I followed everyone's gaze and looked up I saw that he was already on top of the bungee crane. He was being kitted up for the jump by three of the Canadians. I suddenly remembered how pissed they'd all been when I'd last spoken to them at the hospitality tent. That made me feel even more uncomfortable.

The bloke in shades swung round.

"Is everything set?"

Ed panned quickly from Prince Charles to the Sheik.

"Fine," he said, with an unconvincing smile.

The bloke stared at him before turning round and giving the thumbs up to the bloke in the bush. The bloke in the bush gave the thumbs up to a bloke in a raincoat. The bloke in the raincoat spoke into his lapel and, a few seconds later, a bloke with a machine gun came up to Prince Charles and whispered something in his ear before stepping back and giving the thumbs up to the bloke standing next to the Sheik at the top of the crane. The bloke at the top of the crane gave the thumbs up to the bloke who was standing next to Ed.

"Okay son," he said. "Start rolling."

The camera had been rolling for at least three minutes but Ed wasn't going to tell him that. He gave an elaborate thumbs up sign. The bloke didn't think it was funny.

The Sheik stepped up to the jumping platform. He was waving his arms around like a fool. I gripped the wooden rail of the podium.

This was going to go wrong.

I must have seen the tape hundreds of times.

The Sheik swallow dives off the crane without any sense of hesitation. If you watch in slow motion you can see that he's grinning. It's as if he's tasting freedom for the first time after years of bodyguards, food-tasters, servants and full-time grovellers. He's flying, arms outstretched, like a mobile crucifix. With the right kind of music, Clannad or something, it could look beautiful.

At the proper speed though, it's all over in a flash.

He dives. He flies. He hits the ground like a sack.

When he bounces up from the impact his head is the wrong way round and his brain is hanging from a nearby tree. Things get blurry for a bit as Ed zooms in. Blokes appear from everywhere.

"Oh fucking hell!"

That's the one next to us. His voice is distorted. When CNN showed it they bleeped him out. The last thing we see is a superb shot of Prince Charles taking off his Ray-bans. There's blood all over his shirt and he's pushed out of frame by the bloke with the machine gun.

That's it.

Twenty-five seconds which *The Sunday Times* described as "the most remarkable piece of visual documentation since the Zapruder footage." For me though, the most remarkable thing was that it was ever seen at all. I stood at the front of the podium next to the bloke. He was screaming into his walkie-talkie. Down below there was a scrum of blokes around the Sheik's body. One bloke was trying to get the brain down from the tree with a stick. Suddenly the bloke standing next to me swings round. He sees Ed is gone.

"Where is he?"

"What?"

"Don't fucking mess with me pal!"

He whips out the pistol and presses the cold barrel into my ear.

"Where's your mate? Where's that tape?"

"I don't know!"

He's got me in an arm lock and I feel as if I'm going to snap. He lets go.

He checks the camera. The tape is missing.

"Shit!"

He kicks the tripod over.

"Shit! Shit! SHIT!"

He wipes his brow with the back of his hand. Then he presses a red button on his walkie-talkie.

"Seal the area. I don't want anyone leaving the park. Do you understand? Fucking no one!"

He comes over to me again and presses the cold barrel of his pistol into my forehead. I hear a loud click.

"You're dead meat...boyo!"

I get a warm feeling and I realize I've wet myself.

Ed got away. In the confusion he took the tape out of the camera and made a dash for the nearest exit. No one stopped him. Outside the park there was a row of taxis waiting to take some of the catering staff home. Ed hopped into the first in line and, when the driver objected, Ed gave him a hundred quid in tenners.

"Porthcawl. Now!"

Nobody would dream of looking for him there.

He rented a room in a B&B and phoned ITN. He told them what he had. God knows how they understood him. ITN took his number. At first they thought he was a nutter but when they found out about the security and media blackout at the Theme Park they realized something was up and they got back on the phone pronto. They sent a car from London and Ed was whisked away.

He arrived at ITN. He showed them the tape.

They were stunned.

They wanted it.

The cheque book came out.

"A hundred grand."

Ed shook his head.

"A hundred and fifty grand."

Ed shook his head.

"Two hundred grand."

Ed shook his head.

"Okay, a quarter of a million. But that's our final offer."

Ed shook his head.

They couldn't believe it.

"Look son. What the hell do you want?"

Ed sat back in his chair with a smile.

"A job."

The newspapers loved it.

SHEIK SHRIEKS IN HORROR said *The Mirror*.

SHORT SHARP SHEIK SHOCK said *The Sun*.

The Times even featured an editorial calling for the immediate banning of all fairground and Theme Park bungee jumps. All the papers featured stills from the video.

Ed had been clever. He'd taken a hundred grand in cash, a job as a trainee cameraman and a royalty deal. Considering that an edited version of the tape was shown all over the world during the days that followed Ed must have become a millionaire in less than a week.

I was questioned by MI5.

They took me to a big house somewhere in Surrey and interrogated me for three days. They didn't seem to know why they were doing this. I suppose it was a face-saving exercise. In the end they drove me back to Wales in a Jag and placed an agent in the flat for a fortnight just in case Ed tried to make contact. The agent was as confused as me. He reckoned that his bosses simply wanted to duff Ed up for making them look like prats. Both of us agreed that Ed hadn't done anything illegal.

The agent's name was Roger and he said he'd once looked after Salman Rushdie. We got on well. He loved my mum's lemon sponge cake and he took down the recipe for his wife. Sometimes we went for a pint in The Flying Fox and he even did a spot of babysitting for my sister. When he got his orders to leave my dad drove him to the station and we all shook hands on the platform. I asked him for his address in London and he presented me with his card. It said Roger Mills. Painter & Decorator.

Security apparently.

Prince William was taken out of Eton for a term and sent to a farm in New Zealand. No one from the Royal Family commented on the Sheik's death. Everyone expected The Queen to say something during her Christmas Message but she didn't. She just said it had been a very good year for the Commonwealth.

I moved out of the flat above the Rediffusion showroom and went back to live with my parents.

One day I received a letter with a Turkish stamp on it. Inside there was a note. It said 'Old Mill'.

It was from Ed.

I went to the Old Mill and knocked on the door. Perry appeared. He'd lived there for as long as I could remember. When Ed and me had been kids he'd often taken us inside for some of his home-made raspberry squash.

"Oh hello," he said. "There's a letter here for you."

I opened it.

"Not bad news I hope?"

"No," I said. "It's okay."

Inside there were tan post-dated cheques amounting to a quarter of a million pounds.

I opened ten separate accounts and paid in my cheques at weekly intervals. I don't know why I did this but it seemed sensible. I didn't tell anyone about the money and the first withdrawal was a cheque for five thousand pounds which I sent to my uncle. I told him we were now quits.

I never saw Ed again.

I did get a phone call though. It was about a year after the events at the Theme Park.

"It's me."

"Hi."
"You okay?"
"Yeah."
"The letter?"
"Yeah, I got it. Thanks."
There was an uncomfortable pause.
"Ed, where are you?"
"Kosovo."
"Is it good?"
"Yeah, great."
There was another pause.
"Gotta go," he said.
"Ed?"
"Yeah?"
"Are you happy now?"
"Yes. I'm really happy."
I smiled.
It was the longest sentence he'd ever said.

V

VILLA NELLCÔTE

Sometimes I could hear the music. It was in the very walls somehow. In the floor and the roof. How many times had I woken up in the middle of the night during the month or so since I arrived? I'd lost count. And by now I'd become accustomed to it. The sax of Bobby Keyes, Bill Wyman's bass, Keith's guitar and Charlie's drums. Still reverberating. Ghostly and echoing. 1971. That's when they'd been here. Over forty years ago now. Having come over to France to avoid a tax bill large enough to swamp a small country like Luxembourg or Portugal. This is where they recorded *Exile on Main Street*, the last good album they made before they transformed themselves into some kind of ridiculous pantomime on the world stage – Mick in a tracksuit, Keith looking like a lost chimpanzee, Bill bored (as usual) and Charlie looking as if he just wanted to go home. The old walls were canvas absorbing the music like paint. That's what I heard almost every night. The rhythm. The Mississippi Delta blues filtered through Dartford and recreated here in France. Here at Villa Nellcôte.

"You'll get used to it Didier."

That's what Marcel had said before he left for New York. And when was that? June? Early July? I couldn't remember. But I could remember his words as he'd placed the coffee down on the patio table and lit another Marlboro.

"Men mostly. Hell, you know the type. Bearded, plump...middle aged. There at the gates in Stones t-shirts and a Pentax or a Canon round their necks like obscene trophies."

I'd smiled. Marcel had smiled back. But the two of us knew why I was there. The tangible sadness covered us like a blanket.

"What do you tell them?"

"Nothing," said Marcel, as if I'd asked the most stupid question in the world. "I just ignore them."

"Right."

"Of course they'll offer you money. Especially the Americans." Marcel turned to English adopting a near-perfect American accent. "Hey buddy, you wanna show me round this place? I just wanna see where the Stones hung out. I've come all the way from Wisconsin. I've got fifty dollars here."

Marcel smiled again. Shook his head. Sucked on his Marlboro. He sipped his coffee and looked out on the garden. Then at me. "Will you be okay here do you think?"

"Yes."

"I wouldn't have asked but Mme Folliere and her daughter have gone to Switzerland and Mr Vallebriand is down in Antibes. I'm the only one here, and now I have to go over to see Sam in Queens."

"No problem," I said.

"The only time this happened before was two years ago. The decision then was to bring in an ex-policeman from Nice to guard the place. But he ended up stealing some diamonds belonging to Mme Folliere. That's why we need someone trustworthy and dependable to look after the place whilst everyone's away."

"And you thought of me?"

"Why not? You're not likely to steal diamonds are you? And you did use to be a security guard after all."

"That was a long time ago."

Marcel raised his arms as if to say 'so what'.

"But I'm grateful to you Marcel. Seriously. And a month or two in this place will be a real tonic after what you've been through."

"I guess."

Marcel nodded. He crushed the Marlboro in the ashtray and blew smoke like a dragon. He looked at me uncertainly.

"Has she phoned?"

I shook my head. Marcel nodded again. A car beeped from the road and Marcel checked his Rolex.

"I've got to go."

He stood up. So did I. We kissed on both cheeks.

"Text me if there's a problem."

"There won't be."

Marcel smiled. Picked up his bag. Ran down the steps to the gates and raised his hand. The wheels of the taxi crackled on the gravel. After a few minutes the birds kicked in again.

I was on my own.

I got married too soon. Of course I knew that now. Thirty. What kind of age was that? To promise to be faithful to one woman for the rest of your life when you've yet to taste enough of the wild fruit of life? What Andre had told me on the eve of my wedding day had been right.

"Didier, listen. When you're on your own no woman will look at you. But as soon as you're married they sense it somehow and they're drawn to you. You'll see, my friend. You'll see."

Within six months I'd been unfaithful. A business trip to Marseilles. Hotel room. The pretty girl at the bar had been expecting her boyfriend but he'd never turned up. One glass of wine became three. Then four. Next thing I knew we were in bed. She was the first. But there were quite a few opportunities for business trips back then. It was as if there was some kind of knot inside me that was impossible to untie. Every time I did it I felt that perhaps this was the one – the one who would finally loosen the knot and set me free. No more would I be cursed to follow up every cute smile from every pretty girl in every bar.

But that knot remained. If anything it got tighter.

"Hey buddy! You in there?"

He'd been rattling the gates for over fifteen minutes. I was still in my pyjamas as I peeped through the curtains. Fat, bearded guy wearing a baseball cap with 'Broncos' written on it. Naturally, he was in a Stones 'tongue' t-shirt.

"I know you're in there man, I can see you!"

My heart missed a beat. I stepped back and sat on the bed. I glanced at the World Map on my wall. There were little blue stickers on some of the countries. Five over France. Three on Germany. Fifteen across America. Six on Brazil. Eight over England. One on Wales.

"You gotta let me in buddy! I got money. You want cash? I got dollars or Euros man. Come on! Gimme a break here!"

He rattled the gates for another fifteen minutes. Then after cursing me and calling me every name under the sun, he kicked the gate, spat through the grilles and phoned Nice for a taxi.

"Wow! You actually live here?"

"Well," I said, in my best English as I closed the heavy cellar door behind me, "I'm looking after the place."

"Wow," repeated the girl, gazing around the historic basement. She nudged her friend. "Hey Angie, look. This is where the Stones recorded *Exile*."

Her voice echoed around the room. Of course there's nothing left now. No amps. No guitars. Gram Parsons is dead. Mick Taylor left. Bill too. Jagger and Richards have argued and Charlie still wants to go home.

"I was named after the song," said Angie, as her companion walked around the room as if she was in an exhibition area which had once held some priceless art.

"Is that so?" I said. She was the third Angie I'd met during my time at Nellcôte. "Interesting."

Angie nodded and chewed her gum. Her hair is long, thick and blonde. Strangely enough she reminds me a little of Mick Taylor. There's an innocence to her somehow.

"But I don't like the Stones. I prefer Eminem. But I'm here with my sister Mary-Louise because she loves them. I actually think she'd prefer to be called Angie. But I wouldn't want to be called Mary-Louise. It's so trashy. Don't you think?"

"Have you travelled far?"

"Phoenix."

"Hot."

"Can be. We're travelling through Europe right now before going to college. I'm going to UCLA to do film in the fall and Mary-Louise is going to Chicago. Chicago. Where else?"

I smile. She smiles back.

"And it was her idea to come here I suppose?"

"What do you think?"

She chewed her gum and looked around.

"So what's the deal with this place?"

"I'm just looking after the place while the owner's away."

"Sounds like a blast."

"Sometimes."

"And you make money?"

"I don't make any money. It's just a favour. For a friend."

"Well, I sure hope it's worth it."

Mary-Louise came back.

"So cool," she said, her eyes as wide as an owl's, "I can't believe I'm standing in the same room where Mick and Keith sang 'Sweet Virginia'! It's amazing! You sure you don't want any money for this, Didier?"

"No, not at all."

"But I'm so thankful. We're both thankful. Aren't we Angie?"

An hour later they both waved at me from the gate. I smiled from the bedroom and waved back. After the taxi arrived to take them away I opened the drawer by the bed, took out two blue stickers and placed both on Phoenix.

"Someone to help around the house, that's all."

It hadn't been my idea. We didn't need any help. There were only three of us – me, my wife Monique and our daughter Simone. Now Monique wanted an au pair. Of course I knew the real reason why. At breakfast one morning I came out with it. I cleared my throat and put the newspaper down.

"Just because Estelle across the road has an au pair you feel you need one too. That's the real story here isn't it?"

"Don't be so ridiculous! Do you really think I'm as superficial as that?"

"Well, perhaps not. But…"

"Who cleans this house Didier? Eh? Answer me that! Who washes all the clothes and makes sure Simone's got enough money for the school bus? Who has to fetch her home if she's sick in class? Me Didier! That's who! And, just in case you've forgotten, I've also got a part-time job!"

So the interviews began. A seemingly endless parade of beautiful girls from every corner of Europe. All of them eager to improve their French and to spend some time with a real French family. And, naturally enough, out of all these wondrous angels, Monique had to go and choose that fat and coarse girl from Wales.

"You thought I was fat to begin with."

"Don't be silly Liz."

"And what was that other word you used? Coarse. That was it. I heard you arguing one night."

She sat on the edge of the bed and smiled coquettishly.

"But it was clear from your face what you thought of me then. I could see it on your face. Men are so easy to read. Like Mills and fucking Boon."

"Mills and what?"

She rose and held the basque up to her body. Checked herself in the mirror. And then turned to me.

"Are you sure Monique won't mind?"

"She's never worn it. Too big she said."

"Great! Thanks!"

"Sorry."

"I forgive you."

"Your French is improving."

"Do you fancy another Welsh lesson?"

"If the third is as good as the first two why not?"

"Tut tut. Didier is such a naughty boy."

"Come here."

"Monique is bound to find us one afternoon."

"Don't worry. She's never home until after six on a Wednesday. And Simone is at her grandmother's in Juan les Pins. Come. I'm desperate for my Welsh lesson."

Hotel after hotel. Town after town. Only this time there was no chance of going home. And now when I went down to the bars all the young girls avoided me. I knew why of course. I was single again.

The Samsung vibrated in my pocket. Marcel Lamont.

"Hi Marcel."

"You still stuck in that shit hotel?"

"I'm thinking of writing a guide book."

"I've got an offer for you. Are you there?"

"Yes."

"Good. I can't bear to see an old friend rolling round the Riviera like a hobo. Come and see me tomorrow."

"Are you still living in that Nellcôte palace?"

Marcel's laughter crackled the Samsung's speakers.

"It's no palace Didier. As you'll see for yourself tomorrow."

They were still there. I peeped through the curtains again. Sixteen of them. Maybe more. All of them standing perfectly still and gazing up at the window. Of course they knew I was there but, unlike the Americans and the Germans, the Japanese didn't like to be bold. Half an hour. That's how long they'd been there. Men unfortunately, all of them. A blue sticker over Tokyo would have been nice but that island remained untarnished on the map, for now at least. Why didn't they press the buzzer? Or shake the gate? Or even shout something? Watching them all just stand there was really freaky. Part of me felt like opening the window and shouting at them all to fuck off back to Yokohama or wherever just to get some kind of reaction. But no. Like them I was too polite. Eventually their touring bus arrived and they all filed back on, one by one. Some took final photos.

I flopped onto the bed and listened as the bus's engine disappeared down the lane. Birdsong.

Then the buzzer on the gate.

"Shit!"

I sat up and went over to the window expecting to see a stray Japanese bloke that had been left behind by mistake. But no.

It was Monique.

"So this is where you came to hide is it?"

She looked around the bedroom with distaste.

"Not to hide exactly. Marcel asked me to look after the place for a while, that's all. As a favour. I think he knew how bad things were. You know, moving from one dingy hotel to another."

"And we all know whose fault that was don't we?"

Silence. A car whooshed by outside. A world away. Further than Jupiter. Monique clocked the map on the wall.

"Been busy I see."

"It's not what you think."

"I'm not an idiot Didier. I've been with you long enough. I reckon I know you pretty well by now. America in the lead I see."

I cleared my throat.

"Marcel asked me to look after the place because of my security background…"

"Oh Didier! Don't tell me Marcel swallowed that crap about you having been a security guard? You never worked in security in your life! You were a teacher. And a pretty shit teacher too come to that. But no, poor old Didier had to pretend that he was up to something far more exciting. What was it when we first met? You told me you'd just left the Foreign Legion. And that you'd also worked for a while at NASA. I was a naïve young fool to begin with Didier – just like those little blue stickers I'm sure. But I'm not a fool anymore. So are you ready to come home or what?"

"Home? But…"

Monique sighed.

"Not for my sake. For Simone's. We can sleep in separate rooms, for now at least. Then we can see how things go. But you've got to stop chasing all these other women, do you understand? From now on I want this to be a proper marriage. A new beginning."

I nodded. Slowly I felt my entire body unwinding, almost as if there were little fingers inside me loosening the knots that had held me prisoner.

"And you can start by taking that stupid map down and phoning that fat bitch from Wales. I know you've arranged to meet her in Nice next month. But that's all over now. Do you hear me Didier?" She handed me her phone. "Now Didier. Call her."

I swallowed hard. Dialled the number. Listened as the numbers fell into place with beeps and crackles. Then the ringing. The click.

"Hi Liz?"

"Didier?"

"Listen. I've got something to say…"

VI

SHORT CUT

BEHIND ME there were six cows who swished their tails whenever flies buzzed around their bums. Then there was the farmhouse. Behind the farmhouse was a barn and three fields which belonged to Mr Deacon. The gate on which I was sitting belonged to him too. So did the cows. Behind the three fields was a road and a new housing estate where some of my friends lived. Behind them lay the city. Mr Deacon did not own the city. The city was full of cars and buses which stopped at pelican crossings whenever pedestrians pushed a button. When the amber light flashed they continued with their journey. Cars went into multi-storey car parks and buses went into depots. That was the city. It was loud and full of smoke. Some of the buildings were almost black but nobody seemed to mind very much. Behind the city was the airport and behind the airport was the rest of the world. I'd read a book once which said that the world was over a hundred million years old. It was written by a man called Patrick Moore. He said that nobody really understood why dinosaurs became extinct although there were many plausible theories. I'd looked at the back-flap of the book's jacket and worked out that Patrick Moore was fifty-three when the first publication appeared. Mr Deacon was sixty-one and the city was a hundred and twenty. The cows were about four and the flies only lived for twenty four hours. I was fourteen and the time was two-thirty. I glanced down the road and saw Daniel.

"Hi," he shouted. "Been here long?"

Daniel lived in the middle of the woods because his mother liked trees. She cut some of them down with a chain-saw and dragged them into a studio where she turned them into sculptures which sold for lots of money. The first time I stayed there for the weekend surprised me because the house had been full of well-dressed men who had cameras and notebooks. It looked odd because Daniels's mum was so scruffy. Her head was shaved like a convict's and she nearly always wore heavy army boots. Daniel told me it was because the work was dangerous. If she had long hair it might get caught in the lathe and if she wore plimsolls something might fall on her feet and crush them. It all made sense but she still looked slightly fearsome. Not that the well-dressed men seemed too bothered. All they were interested in were the sculptures. When they left, Daniel's mum clapped her hands and drove us into the city for an Indian meal. She'd just sold five sculptures to a New York gallery and Daniel told me that the deal had been worth thousands. That was the first time I realized that Daniel and his mum were rich. Up until then I'd even pitied them a little. There was no telly in the house and the car was a banger. In the bathroom there was a large hole in the floor and the kitchen was full of old milk bottles. They'd never been rinsed and the insides were encrusted with sour milk which had gone yellow and very smelly. On the way back from the Indian restaurant that evening I remember asking Daniel if his mum was going to use any of the New York money to buy a proper house. She overheard and began a laugh that lasted for almost a minute and a half.

"About the usual," I said.

By now Daniel was leaning on the gate and staring at the cows. He had a thin blade of grass in his mouth.

"I thought we'd go to Well's Wood today," he said.

"What's in Well's Wood?"

"Trees," he said, with a smile.

I paused for a bit before leaping off the gate.

"Alright," I said. "Lead the way."

Daniel knew his way round the countryside. In the city he was a bit of a dead loss because it was full of streets and corner-shops. Whenever we went for a lunchtime wander during the school break it would always be Daniel who got lost or looked bemused. He didn't know how to behave there. It was as if he was a tourist in a land whose language he didn't understand. Because he never watched telly he was uncertain as to which sweets he should buy and, usually, he ended up with whatever we got. Smoking was strange to him too. His mum had never threatened him with a bollocking if he ever got caught so the danger element was missing. Even when Mickey Staples found some dope it meant nothing to Daniel. Mickey rolled a joint and offered it round but when it came to Daniel he just looked at it for a second before refusing. He did it without any hint of superiority and nobody accused him of being chicken. Everyone respected Daniel in a peculiar kind of way. Even the teachers liked him, particularly Miss Cairn who, as the art teacher, had quickly sussed out who Daniel's mum was and who no doubt hoped for some special favours. In Daniel's first week at our school he was taken to the front of the Still Life class and introduced as the son of a famous artist. Everyone had blank expressions and Daniel was blushing with embarrassment. He tried to wriggle free but Miss Cairn never let go of his shoulders. She stood behind him like a clamp. When the speech was over Daniel ran to his seat and I saw that he was shaking.

"What the hell's that?"

"It's a camera," said Daniel. "Mum wants me to take some photos of trees in Well's Wood."

"For a sculpture is it?"

Daniel shrugged his shoulders.

It didn't take long before Miss Cairn went on the offensive. She brought a large wooden box to school one day and as we were all filing out for our morning break she called Daniel back for a couple of minutes. When he came out again he was carrying Miss Cairn's box. I asked him what was in it and he told me that it contained paintings which Miss Cairn had done as a student. She wanted Daniel's mum to give a professional opinion as to their quality. Daniel had tried to explain that his mother was very busy but Miss Cairn just smiled. She said she was willing to wait and so Daniel was forced to take the wooden box with him on the school bus home. He looked really worried and told me that Miss Cairn had chosen the worst possible time to approach his mum with paintings because the television people had left a hell of a mess. Things were chaotic, he said. His mum had had to start spring-cleaning the whole place. He tapped the wooden box with his hand and said that Miss Cairn would probably have to wait a bit longer than she'd anticipated.

Daniel was dropped off at Looper's Edge. From there he walked up the narrow road which led through the woods until he came to a clearing. Here there was a washing line and a clutch of oil drums which had been painted white although nobody knew why. There was also a small hut. It was about twenty yards away from the house and Daniel's mum hardly ever used it. Daniel opened the door and pushed Miss Cairn's box into a corner. It would be safe there for the time being.

"She's gone to the city," said Daniel, "otherwise she'd take them herself. I told her I'd do it so she handed me the camera. She knows I've been dying to play with it for ages."

We all knew that Miss Cairn lived alone in a terraced house because Mickey Staples kept an eye on her. Mickey lived in the city too. He was a born snooper and he would share his findings with us during lunchtime breaks. According to him, Miss Cairn spent most of her time in front of the television although two nights a week were taken up by her private art classes. Two old women came on Tuesday evenings. They carried Daler-boards and duffel bags. Miss Cairn led them into the back room and made them a cup of tea whilst they got in the mood. Then a vase of flowers was placed on the table and the old ladies were told to paint it. At half-past nine Miss Cairn checked the results and made them another cup of tea. They chatted until ten and then the old women packed up their gear. Miss Cairn collected the money on the way out and told them to take care on the dark streets. She would then go inside and switch on the television.

Her other customer was Mr Henderson and he came on Thursdays. Miss Cairn could hear him coming before he even reached the street corner because he carried his paintbrushes in a biscuit tin which rattled as he walked. On this signal she would open the cocktail cabinet where all the sherry was kept. Both were mad on sherry. Mr Henderson was welcomed by a large glass and by the time he started painting he'd be grinning and nodding like a clown. Hislesson centered itself on a large canvas which Mickey Staples said was covered with grey paint. He also said that he could overhear their conversation and at first we had been really excited because we were hoping that something scandalous was going on. It was very disappointing to learn that all they talked about was aeroplanes.

Mr Henderson had been in the RAF for most of his life and, after that, he had worked at the local flying school. He was always promising to take Miss Cairn up in his Gypsy Moth but that promise had never been fulfilled. However hard she tried, Miss Cairn couldn't pin him down to a specific date. She hinted and she grovelled. She knew that he still liked to be called Squadron Leader so she did. She even allowed him to smoke his pipe in the lounge. On his previous birthday she had baked him an enormous fruit cake but the sacrifice had come to nothing. At ten o'clock Mr Henderson would pay Miss Cairn and thank her for all the sherry. He would sometimes make a note in his diary to remind himself about the Gypsy Moth before saying goodnight and heading for home, his biscuit tin fading slowly in the distance.

That was Miss Cairn's routine and we all thought it was really boring. Mickey however had persisted with his snooping and one day he surprised us by saying that things had changed. Mr Henderson still came round on Thursday evenings but Miss Cairn no longer called him Squadron Leader or pestered him about the Gypsy Moth. For weeks she had been rifling through cupboards and drawers for the paintings she had done as a student. She gathered them carefully until there was a large pile on the settee. She went through them one by one until the final selection had been made and then she packed them tightly into a wooden box which had once held a set of China. Everything was prepared and she let out a long sigh of relief. She was completely unaware of the fact that she'd forgotten Mr Henderson's birthday. Forgotten to bake him a fruit cake.

"It's a Pentax," said Daniel. "Automatic wind-on and all."

"Automatic what?"

"Wind-on. It means I can take lots of pictures very quickly."

"Seems a pity to waste it on trees."

"Trees can be interesting sometimes," said Daniel. "At first they all look the same but the closer you get the more fascinating they are."

The television people had been at Daniel's house for just over a month. They came at nine every morning and finished filming at four. The director was a man called Roger Hampshire who seemed to know a lot about Daniel's mum and a lot about sculpture in general. Apparently he was quite famous but to Daniel and me he was just a bearded man in a floppy jacket. It was fun watching them. The first couple of days were the best because Daniel's mum was in a good mood. The atmosphere was calm and nobody got on each other's nerves. It was on the fifth day that things began to get a bit tricky because Roger Hampshire decided he needed more lighting and twenty people arrived in two silver vans. From then it was chock-a-block. There were wires and leads and lights everywhere. People bumped into each other all the time and Daniel's mum accused Roger Hampshire of turning her house into a circus. Strange technicians moved in and out of her front room as if they'd just bought it and the studio was impossible to get into. Even the small hut where nobody ever went was filled with boxes of spare light bulbs.

Daniel's mum went along with everything that was asked of her purely because she wanted the whole thing completed as soon as possible. What annoyed her most of all were the alterations in her studio. It had changed beyond recognition with lights, cameras, deflective screens and microphones. Her sculptures had been moved as if they were nothing more than odd pieces of furniture. She said she felt useless and desperately wished for the day when Hampshire and his crew left.

When that day came however it was obvious that her troubles were far from over. The place was a complete mess. Muddy footprints covered her studio floor and scraps of paper were strewn across her workbenches. It took three days for her to restore the studio to its normal condition. After that she tidied up the entire house and picked up loose pieces of litter from around the white-painted oil drums. Whilst she was there she investigated the small hut. Inside there were two boxes of broken light bulbs which had been half-hidden underneath a plastic raincoat. There was also a large wooden box which had been pushed into the corner. She took all three boxes to the edge of the wood and dumped them into a pool. They sank to the bottom and Daniel's mum sat down on a tree trunk to catch her breath. After a while she noticed that the surface of the pool seemed to carry faint traces of paint.

"Wouldn't it be more fun to draw them?"

Daniel wrinkled up his nose.

"No," he said. "You notice them too much then. You get to know your subject too well."

I didn't understand what he was on about so I asked him to explain.

"It's difficult," he said, "but take my mum for instance. One day she found a beautiful piece of wood but couldn't think what to do with it. In the end she just sliced a tiny mark in the side with a sharp knife." He looked at me hopefully. "Oh dear. I haven't explained it very well."

Mr Henderson had been looking forward to receiving his birthday cake. During one of his Thursday evening sessions he had searched the kitchen while Miss Cairn had gone upstairs. Tins were carefully judged for weight and cupboards were opened with the dexterity of a burglar. He knew that Miss Cairn was crafty. She was probably fully aware that it was the eve of his birthday and, as was equally probable, wanted to keep him in suspense for a while. Mr Henderson was perfectly willing to participate in her little game. She knew he was unmarried and that nobody else would have baked him a cake. She knew so much about him. Even which sherry he preferred. As Miss Cairn came down the stairs he returned to the lounge and lit his pipe. He smiled a cagey smile and waited for the end of the evening.

When the truth dawned on him he was stunned. Mickey Staples said that his face went white as he was led to the front door with the realization that there wouldn't be a fruit cake that year. There wasn't even a card. On his way home he stopped at The Dog and Bounty and ordered a double brandy. It was the first time he had been in the pub and all the regulars eyed the rattling tin with suspicion. He exchanged a few vacant nods before taking his drink to the corner table. The regulars at the bar stared at him for a bit but they soon lost interest when another of their mates walked in. Squadron Leader Henderson stayed until closing time. Nobody came up to him and offered him a drink. Nobody in the whole world cared that it was the eve of his sixty-fourth birthday.

"Lift the wire," said Daniel. "And be careful because it's very sharp."

I had been daydreaming for a while and was amazed to see that we had arrived at Well's Wood so soon. Daniel had probably taken a short cut. I fingered the barbed wire with trepidation.

"Just lift it," said Daniel. "You'll be fine."

I did as I was told and followed Daniel into the dark wood.

"That'll do to start with," he said, pointing to a gnarled old tree. He knelt down on one knee and raised the camera to his face. He took aim and fired. It wasn't long until the whole roll of film had been used up. About ten minutes in fact. Daniel then walked up to me and swung the camera over his shoulder.

"There," he said. "Finished."

VII

THE SAD TALE OF "CRAZY" LUKE DOBER

THE NAME "Crazy" Luke Dober doesn't mean much to anyone these days but, back in Alabama at the beginning of the sixties, this guy was pretty famous. Unfortunately he was famous for all the wrong reasons.

He was famous for being the unluckiest man in pop.

"Crazy" Luke Dober was certainly talented, no one would have argued about that. He was the alto saxophonist in Little John and the Sweethearts (one of the most promising bands in Alabama at the turn of the decade) but, after two solid years of gigging in New York and L.A. in the hope of attracting the attention of one of the major recording companies – without any success – "Crazy" Luke decided to give up the sax and he returned to Alabama to try to find a job and settle down.

A month after he'd started working at Big Jeff's Oldsmobile and Used Car Bonanza in Albertstown he heard the news that Little John and the Sweethearts had signed a deal with RCA Victor and that they were at number 25 in the charts with a song called "Tell Me You Need (My Good Lovin')". Upon hearing this news, "Crazy" Luke jumped into a 1954 Buick Special (with a Nailhead V8 engine) which was lying in the yard, drove it at high speed towards Dalton Bridge (attracting the attention of the Highway Patrol as he did so), jumped out, leaving the door flapping like an elephant's ear, and – without even troubling himself to look down – he dived into the river to put an end to his miserable and unlucky life.

Unfortunately, his legendary bad luck even extended to his ambition of committing suicide because the water levels in the river were unnaturally low that day and "Crazy" Luke landed head first in five feet of thick mud. After being hosed down by a local farmer he was given a fine of $150 and fired from Big Jeff's Oldsmobile and Used Car Bonanza.

Living was hard. Every day he heard people in the bars and the stores talking excitedly about the success of the local band – Little John and the Sweethearts (number 10 on the *Billboard* chart by now and shortly to make a coast-to-coast appearance on the *Ed Sullivan Show*). Yes, Little John and the Sweethearts had succeeded whilst "Crazy" Luke – arguably the most talented member of the band – had to stand in line outside the Temperance Mission on the outskirts of Albertstown. Sometimes one of the other down-and-outs would recognize him.

"Say Buddy, ain't you the guy who used to play sax with Little John's band?"

"No, not me."

"Don't shit me man! I saw you at the Ritzo every Saturday night for two fucking years! Hey everybody, look who we got here! This is the shit-for-brains who left Little John and the Sweethearts just before they scored a hit!"

It didn't matter how high he pulled up the collar on his coat, everyone recognized "Crazy" Luke and everyone pointed and laughed.

"There he goes, the unluckiest dude in the world!"

LOCAL BAND ON TOP OF THE CHARTS!

That was the headline in the following week's issue of the *Albertstown and Meadowville Gazette* and, as he looked at the accompanying picture of his old band mates sipping champagne with Elvis Presley out in Hollywood, "Crazy" Luke decided that he should, once again, end it all. Only this time there would be no fuck up's.

He went home, went to the garage and reached for the rifle that had belonged to his Grandaddy. It was a Winchester Model 1912 and it weighed a ton. It was always kept loaded to try to deter the coyotes which sometimes came round to scavenge stuff from the trash.

Unfortunately – or fortunately, depending on how you look at it – as he walked up to the Winchester Model 1912 on the rack, "Crazy" Luke trod on a garden rake that had been placed against one of the cupboards. The only thing it took to transform this innocent gardening tool into a clinical and semi-deadly weapon was "Crazy" Luke's size nine shoe.

As he stood on it, the rake's progress was cruel and swift – the wooden handle shot forwards and whacked "Crazy" Luke in the face, knocking him to the floor like a rookie boxer. And that's where he lay, unconscious, for three hours, draped by a red scarf of blood. When he came round there was a young boy standing over him.

"What do you want kid?" asked "Crazy" Luke.

"This is for you." he said, holding out an envelope.

"What is it?"

"Telegram. Western Union. Hey, do you know your face is bleeding?"

"Crazy" Luke sat up, gave the kid a dollar and sent him away.

"Shit!" he said, on reading the telegram, "I don't believe it!" He stood up and began to laugh. "I don't fucking believe it!"

Then – having kicked away the rake – he jigged around the garage like a hillbilly!

The telegram itself was only three sentences long and it said that "Crazy" Luke's Aunt Sally from Spring Falls, Montana (an Aunt he had never heard of before) had died leaving him – her sole heir – twenty thousand dollars.

The first thing he did with the money was buy a house – 23009 Meadowville – and convert the basement into a recording studio. It was pretty basic by today's standards – one room in the back with three microphones, a piano, some drums and lots of padded cork on the walls to keep down the noise – but at least it was a start. The way "Crazy"

Luke saw it, perhaps Little John and the Sweethearts may have scored a big number one hit but, from now on, it would be he – "Crazy" Luke Dober – who would be recording a stream of future hits from his own studio and on his own label, Hit-State Records.

Hit-State Records studio was one of the few of its kind in Lee County towards the end of 1963 and, because of this, the place quickly filled up with musicians and singers. The drive at the front of 23009 Meadowville was full of Ford pick-ups, Oldsmobiles and Plymouths, all of them packed to the brim with drums, guitars and amplifiers by bands who had been inspired by the success of Little John and the Sweethearts and who were no doubt hopeful that some of the magic might rub off on them, courtesy of an ex-member of the outfit.

The first release on Hit-State Records was "Good Lovin'" by a young local band called The Cobras. It never got close to a *Billboard* entry but it received a good response locally and was picked up by WB-NBX in Auburn. In all, 238 copies were sold and "Crazy" Luke made a loss. But of course that didn't matter. It was a start. And, besides, there was still plenty of Aunt Sally's money in the bank.

For now at least.

The second big thing "Crazy" Luke bought was a car. By now he'd realized that if we was to emulate the success of someone like Sam Phillips from Sun Records in Memphis with a young truck-driving hillbilly called Elvis Presley staying in Meadowville was not an option. He would have to travel around Lee County, and possibly even further. With this in mind, therefore, he spent $500 on a red, second-hand Studebaker Commander, threw his suitcase in the trunk and hit the road in search of talent.

He went to every night club and dance hall in Lee County but, after three weeks of living in cheap motels and spending a small fortune on gas, "Crazy" Luke decided that it was just another dead end idea. He was never going to find another Elvis. Perhaps there was raw, undiscovered talent in every county and state in the US but, in "Crazy" Luke's mind, Alabama was the exception. All he'd seen during his journey had been a string of second-rate combos with out of tune guitars and countless singers who had the charisma of a paper towel. They had as much chance of being the next Elvis as Yuri Gagarin had of being a cast member of *Rawhide*.

So, one morning, with his dream of being a music mogul lying in tatters (and with less than $800 of Aunt Sally's money left), rather than turn the Studebaker to the left on leaving the motel (in order to see if there were any good groups or singers in Tuskegee, Macon County), "Crazy" Luke turned right.

And headed for home.

As the torrential rain whipped the windshield of the Studebaker, and as the motels and gas stations passed by, "Crazy" Luke Dober realized that he was never going to get his ten minutes in the sun like his old bandmates in Little John and the Sweethearts. He was not going to discover the next Elvis in Lee County, nor even in Macon County. In fact, with his luck, "Crazy" Luke reckoned he wouldn't even discover the next Elvis even if he landed on the hood of the Studebaker that very moment.

But, strangely enough, that was exactly what happened.

As he drove slowly along the main street of Marlonville (a town of around 2,000 people), "Crazy" Luke Dober leant over to change the dial on the radio and in that split second, as he took his eyes off the road, he hit something. Something big. Something big enough to buckle up the hood of the Studebaker. For a second, as he pulled the car over to the sidewalk, "Crazy" Luke thought he must have hit a horse, or some kind of runaway bear.

But then, through the drilling rain, he saw the shape of a man. A big man. Eighteen stone without a doubt. Maybe even heavier. Twenty? However heavy he was, the man's sheer bulk appeared to have protected him from serious injury because he'd stood up and was brushing down his coat as if he'd done no more than trip over a dog.

"Hey," said "Crazy" Luke Dober, running up to him (the last thing he needed right now was a fucking lawsuit!), "you okay buddy?"

"Yeah, I'm fine."

"I didn't see you."

"You're joking right? How could you not see me? The biggest man in town – and the only one who's black!" He shook his head and chuckled. "Most folks round these parts see me coming a mile off!"

"Crazy" Luke Dober was sure he was in trouble. There was no one else around. No one to help him if the big guy turned on him and decided to kill him. The rain hit the tarmac like bullets. Who the fuck went out on a night like this?

With his heart thumping like a bass drum, "Crazy" Luke swallowed hard and tried to rescue the situation. He'd heard of people being left for dead in places like this. Small towns with only one cop.

"Hey listen, you sure you're okay? Do you want me to call you a doctor or anything?"

"No man, I don't need no doctor. And besides, you think a guy like me's got medical cover? Just pass me that thing will you?"

The man was referring to a guitar case. "Crazy" Luke picked it up.

"You a musician?"

"George Morton," said the man, extending his hand and smiling, "although most folks call me 'Tiny'. It's like some kind of joke you understand? Hey, why don't you come and see me play? I've got a gig tonight and I need a little support. See, I lost my job today and now I've just been knocked down by some dude in a Stude. On top of all this it's pissing down a storm and everyone in town is indoors watching *Wagon Train*. You know, sometimes I feel as if the good Lord created bad luck just for me."

"Yeah," said "Crazy" Luke Dober under his breath. "Maybe not just you."

THE BEATLES IN TONYPANDY

The Golden Bronco was a hole but at least it was indoors. By now "Crazy" Luke Dober's soaking shirt was clinging to him like a second skin. But at least he looked better than George "Tiny" Morton. His suit had a series of rips and tears and it had splashes of oil, mud and traces of red paint. It could have been designed by Jackson Pollock.

"What the fuck happened to you?" said the owner. "You look like shit."

"This guy ran me over in his car."

The owner looked at "Crazy" Luke. Then he spat in a bucket and turned back to Tiny.

"Yeah well, you'd better go on and sing. Your audience is waiting."

"Right," said Tiny, glancing at the near-empty bar. "I can see that."

As he watched Tiny plugging in his guitar with a loud and unprofessional crack, "Crazy" Luke Dober's expectations were pretty low and the last thing he needed now, after being soaked to the skin and given the fright of his life, was to hear another shit singer destroying some R&B hits of the day. What he really wanted was to go home, run a bath, drink half a bottle of bourbon and then go to bed. But how could he turn down an invitation from someone he'd almost killed? Saying no to Tiny would have been discourteous, cruel even.

No, in "Crazy" Luke's mind, the best thing to do now was order a Pepsi and stay for a while – three songs maybe – before sneaking off without anyone noticing (although he could see that would be difficult in an half-empty bar). So, with an ice cold Pepsi in his hand, "Crazy" Luke Dober turned his attention to the stage...

...and was completely blown away!

George "Tiny" Morton was a star. This was obvious to "Crazy" Luke Dober even if it wasn't to the other ten people in the Golden Bronco that night. He couldn't believe it. Why wasn't the place heaving? Why weren't people fighting to get in to hear this guy sing? His talent was so natural and astounding. His voice was deep and with a pleasing bluesy edge. This was a cry from the heart of downtrodden America. This was a cry that offered hope and salvation. It was a cry which began with a small spark but which would surely intensify until it would be a fierce inferno raging through America's cultural desert!

Was "Crazy" Luke the only person who could see this?

After finishing his first set George "Tiny" Morton went to the bar and, as usual, ordered himself a Root Beer. He had ten minutes before he was due to begin his second set and, within those ten minutes, he had signed a contract with Hit-State Records (a contract hastily drawn up on the back of a napkin). Then, within three weeks, he was listening back to his recording of "Please Be My Baby" at 23009 Meadowville and smiling as the grinding bass vibrated along the floorboards.

"I tell you, this is a hit!" said "Crazy" Luke Dober, having to shout over the music and spilling some of his bourbon, "sure-fire goddam fucking hit!"

"Well, it does sound sweet, I gotta say."

The early reaction from WB-NBX in Auburn was encouraging too. Previously, "Crazy" Luke Dober had got the distinct impression that the local DJs were spinning Hit-State discs out of some sense of sympathy or pity, but now, with "Please Be My Baby", all that changed. Now all the DJs were crowding round their Dansettes and playing the promo copies over and over again whilst dancing and laughing.

"This is a hit," said Hube Long, one of the most influential DJs on WB-NBX, slapping "Crazy" Luke on the shoulder as if he'd known him all his life. "When can we play it on the show?"

"Any time you like Hube. The disc's out in a week's time. On November 23rd."

"Man, I gotta tell you," said Hube Long, his teeth yellow and his breath stinking of Camels, "that's gonna be your lucky day. This record's going to be a *Billboard* smash!"

The phone in 23009 Meadowville had never been so busy. DJs from as far away as New York and Chicago were ringing up wanting advance copies of "Please Be My Baby" and "Crazy" Luke was running out of stock. He ordered more copies from the pressing plant in Albertstown but, just to be safe – and anticipating a possible million-seller – he also contacted a much bigger plant in Los Angeles (the same one that provided discs for Capitol) to see if they could take over if the song broke into the *Billboard* Top Ten as everyone seemed to predict.

One morning "Crazy" Luke took a call from Jay Stenner from RCA Victor asking questions about Tiny Morton. But, sitting back in his chair and puffing a huge Monte Cristo cigar, "Crazy" Luke Dober had enjoyed telling a Hollywood big shot music mogul that Tiny Morton was not, repeat not, for sale.

On the morning of the 22nd "Crazy" Luke Dober woke up late. And the way he saw it, who could blame him? The past few weeks had been wild. He'd travelled around as many radio stations as he could doing promotion, giving out copies and making sure the DJs played it on heavy rotation prior to release. He'd hired a secretary to deal with all the calls that were coming in and he'd even gone to an Albertstown lawyer to redraft the contract with Tiny Morton just in case Jay Stenner came sniffing around again. Of course, he had no objection to selling Tiny to a big label (just like Sam Phillips had done with Elvis) but not just yet. Not until the price had got bigger and it was a more attractive proposition. Not until "Please Be My Baby" had reached number one on the *Billboard* chart.

The first thing he did that morning was make some coffee and click on the radio fully expecting to hear Hube Long playing "Please Be My Baby" (just like he did on every show) and insisting that everyone went out and bought a copy when it finally reached the stores the following day.

But no.

The only thing "Crazy" Luke Dober heard on the radio that day was some guy talking about some bad shit that had gone down in Texas.

Texas?

What the fuck did WB-NBX have to do with Texas?

He returned to WFFX in Lanceton. The reception wasn't quite so clear but the message as the same here too – two rather serious voices discussing Texas.

What the fuck was wrong with the world? Why wasn't America hearing "Please Be My Baby" by Tiny Morton on the day prior to release? Why hadn't the DJs kept their word and placed it on strict rotation? This was a hit! That's what everyone had told him! A sure-fire fucking h –

The phone rang.

"Hello?"

"Hey man," said Tiny, his voice serious and heavy for once, "you heard the news?"

"Well I ain't heard your fucking song that's for sure!"

"Some guy shot the President in Dallas."

It's said that almost everyone in America over the age of 55 are likely to know exactly where they were when they heard the news that John F. Kennedy had been shot. "Crazy" Luke Dober was in his kitchen in his pyjamas.

Within an hour he was in the garden with three empty cans of Budweiser at his feet.

Within a month the bills for the extra copies of "Please Be My Baby" came through the mail.

Within three months The Beatles had appeared on *Ed Sullivan* and changed music forever.

Within five months Lee County Police Department were pulling the body of a male in his mid-thirties from the Chattahoochee River. April 3rd, 1964.

Hardly anyone remembers where they were the day "Crazy" Luke Dober died.

VIII

HANES TRIST
"CRAZY" LUKE DOBER

Tydi enw "Crazy" Luke Dober ddim yn golygu lot fawr dyddia yma ond, yn Alabama ar ddechra'r chwedegau, mi roedd y gŵr yma yn eitha enwog. Yn anffodus roedd o'n enwog am y rhesymau anghywir.

Am fod yn un o'r pobol mwya anlwcus yn y byd pop.

Mi roedd "Crazy" Luke Dober yn foi talentog, doedd neb yn dadla efo hynny. Roedd o'n chwara Alto Sax yng ngrŵp Little John and the Sweethearts (un o fandiau mwya addawol Alabama ar ddechrau'r chwedegau) ond, ar ôl dwy flynedd o gigio o gwmpas Efrog Newydd a Los Angeles, gan obeithio denu sylw un o'r cwmnïau recordiau mawr – heb unrhyw lwc o gwbwl – mi wnaeth "Crazy" Luke benderfynu rhoi'r Alto Sax yn y to a symud yn ôl i Alabama er mwyn ffendio job a setlo i lawr.

Mis ar ôl iddo fo ddechrau yn Big Jeff's Oldsmobile and Used Car Bonanza yn Albertstown gafodd o'r newyddion fod Little John and the Sweethearts wedi arwyddo dêl efo RCA Victor a'u bod nhw yn rhif 25 ar y siartiau gyda chân o'r enw "Tell Me You Need (My Good Lovin')". Ar ôl clywed hyn mi ddringodd "Crazy" Luke i 1954 Buick Special ag injan Nailhead V8 ar yr iard, ei yrru'n wyllt i Dalton Bridge (gan ddenu sylw tri car heddlu), rhedeg allan o'r Buick, gan adael y drws i bendilio fel clust eliffant ac – heb hyd yn oed edrych i lawr – mi gaeodd ei lygaid a neidio i'r afon i roi diwedd, am byth, ar bob dim.

Yn anffodus roedd ei anlwc yn ymestyn i'w obaith o gyflawni hunanladdiad hefyd oherwydd mi roedd y dŵr yn yr afon yn anarferol o isel y diwrnod hwnnw ac fe laniodd mewn pum troedfedd o fwd. Ar ôl cael ei lanhau gan beipen ddŵr oer gan ffarmwr lleol fe gafodd "Crazy" Luke ddirwy o $150 a'r sac o Big Geoff's Oldsmobile and Used Car Bonanza.

Roedd bywyd yn anodd. Bob dydd roedd o'n clywed pawb yn y bariau a'r siopau'n llawenhau yn llwyddiant yng ngrŵp lleol, Little John and the Sweethearts. (Rhif 10 yn y siart *Billboard* erbyn hyn ac yn barod i ymddangos coast to coast ar *The Ed Sullivan Show*.) Mi oedd Little John and the Sweethearts wedi llwyddo tra bod "Crazy" Luke – aelod mwyaf talentog y grŵp, efalla – yn gorfod sefyll mewn rhes am gawl tu allan i'r Temperance Mission ar gyrion Albertstown. Weithia bysa criw o ddynion yn ei adnabod.

"Hei, nid ti oedd y boi oedd yn arfer chwarae'r Alto Sax efo Little John and the Sweethearts?"

"Na, nid fi."

"Paid â malu! Dwi'n dy gofio di! Hei, sbiwch bawb! Sbiwch ar y ffŵl yma! Y ffwl naeth adael Little John and the Sweethearts jyst cyn iddyn nhw gael hit!"

Dim ots pa mor uchel oedd o'n tynnu coler ei got dros ei wyneb roedd pawb yn adnabod "Crazy" Luke ac mi roedd pawb yn pwyntio bys a chwerthin am ei ben.

"Sbiwch arno fo! Y dyn mwya anlwcus yn y byd!"

GRŴP LLEOL AR FRIG Y SIARTIAU.

Dyna oedd y pennawd yn rhifyn yr wythnos ganlynol o'r *Albertstown and Meadowville Ga-*

zette. Wrth weld y llun o aelodau Little John and the Sweethearts yn yfed siampên efo Elvis Presley yn Hollywood dyma "Crazy" Luke yn penderfynu rhoi diwedd ar bethau eto – ond tro yma fasa 'na ddim amheuaeth. Mi aeth o adra a mynd i'r garij i estyn y dryll oedd yn perthyn i'w daid: Winchester Model 1912. Roedd o'n drwm ac mi oedd "Crazy" Luke yn gwbod na fasa fo'n methu tro yma oherwydd roedd y gwn wastad yn llawn bwledi oherwydd y coyotes oedd yn dod rownd i hel bwyd o'r biniau a chreu llanast.

Yn anffodus – neu yn ffodus (mae'n dibynnu sut dach chi'n edrych ar y peth) – wrth iddo fo gamu tuag at y Winchester Model 1912 ar y rac ar y wal mi safodd "Crazy" Luke Dober ar gribin oedd yn gorffwys yn ddiniwed yn erbyn un o'r cypyrddau. Y cwbwl gymerodd hi i droi'r cribin o fod yn offeryn garddio hynaws i arf peryglus a chlinigol oedd troed seis naw "Crazy" Luke Dober.

Wrth iddo sefyll arni roedd ymateb y cribin yn frwnt ac yn chwim. Mi waldiodd y handlan bren "Crazy" Luke Dober ar ei drwyn a'i gnocio i'r llawr fel cadach. A dyna lle fuodd o'n anymwybodol am dair awr mewn sgarff biws o waed. Pan ddoth o at ei hun mi oedd 'na fachgen yn sefyll uwch ei ben.

"Be tisho?" gofynnodd "Crazy" Luke Dober.

"Mae hwn i chdi," medda'r bachgen, gan estyn amlen.

"Be ydi o?"

"Telegram. Western Union. Hei, wyt ti'n gwbod fod dy drwyn yn gwaedu?"

Cododd "Crazy" Luke Dober ar ei eistedd, rhoi doler i'r bachgen a'i yrru i ffwrdd.

"Blydi hel," medda fo, gan ddarllen y telegram. "Fedra i ddim coelio'r peth!" Dyma fo'n codi o'r llawr ac yn chwerthin. "Fedra i ddim... coelio'r peth!!"

Wedyn – ar ôl sicrhau nad oedd y cribin o dan ei draed y tro yma – dyma fo'n dawnsio rownd y garej fel hilbili!

Tair brawddeg gwta o hyd oedd y telegram yn dweud wrth "Crazy" Luke Dober bod ei fodryb Sally o Spring Falls, Montana (modryb nad oedd o rioed wedi clywed amdani o'r blaen) wedi marw a wedi gadael $20,000 iddo fo, Mr Luke Dober – ei hunig nai.

Y peth cynta wnaeth o efo'r arian oedd prynu tŷ – 23009 Meadowville – a troi'r selar yn stiwdio recordio. O'i chymharu â safonau heddiw efalla ei bod hi braidd yn gyntefig – un stafell yn y cefn efo tri meicroffon, piano, dryms a llwyth o deils corc a phacedi wyau ar y waliau er mwyn cadw'r sŵn i lawr – ond o leia mi oedd yn ddechreuad. Y ffordd roedd "Crazy" Luke Dober yn gweld petha, efallai fod Little John and the Sweethearts wedi cyrraedd brig y siartiau ond, o hyn ymlaen, "Crazy" Luke Dober fyddai'n recordio hits y dyfodol yn ei stiwdio fach ac, ar label ei hun, sef label Hit-State Records.

Stiwdio Hit-State Records oedd un o'r ychydig o'i math yn Lee County ar ddiwedd 1963 ac, oherwydd hyn, roedd y lle'n llawn o gantorion a cherddorion o fewn dim. Roedd gardd ffrynt 23009 Meadowville yn frith o Ford pick-ups, Oldsmobiles, a Plymouths – pob un wedi eu pacio i'r ymylon â dryms, amps a gitars, eiddo grŵpiau oedd wedi eu hysbrydoli gan lwyddiant Little John and the Sweethearts ac a oedd yn gobeithio cael rhif un eu hunain.

Y record gynta a ryddhawyd ar Hit-State Records oedd "Good Lovin'" gan grŵp lleol ifanc o'r enw The Cobras. Aeth hi ddim yn agos i'r siartiau *Billboard* ond mi gafodd hi ymateb cynnes yn lleol ac roedd hi i'w chlywed yn eitha amal ar orsaf radio WB-NBX yn Auburn. Gwerthwyd 238 o gopïau i gyd ac mi oedd "Crazy" Luke ar ei golled. Ond doedd dim ots am hynny, wrth gwrs. Roedd digon o arian Anti Sally o Spring Falls ar ôl yn y banc.

Am rŵan o leia.

Yr ail beth mawr i "Crazy" Luke brynu oedd car. Erbyn hyn roedd o wedi sylweddoli os oedd o am efelychu llwyddiant rhwyn fel Sam Phillips o Sun Records yn Memphis efo gyrrwr lori o'r enw Elvis Presley doedd aros yn Meadowville ddim yn opsiwn. Mi fasa raid iddo fo deithio o gwmpas Lee County – ac ymhellach hyd yn oed. Efo hyn mewn golwg, felly, dyma "Crazy" Luke yn gwario $500 ar Studebaker Commander coch ail law, taflu ei ges i'r bŵt a tharo'r lôn i chwilio am dalent.

Aeth o i bob clwb nos a phob dawns yn Lee County ond, ar ôl tair wythnos o fyw mewn motels rhad a gwario ffortiwn ar betrol, dyma "Crazy" Luke Dober yn penderfynu mai breuddwyd ffôl oedd hyn i gyd. Doedd o ddim am ddarganfod ei Elvis. Falla fod 'na dalent amrwd heb ei ddarganfod ym mhob sir a talaith arall yn America ond doedd neb yn Alabama. Y cyfan oedd "Crazy" Luke Dober wedi'i glywed a'i weld yn ystod y daith oedd grwpiau di-nod yn canu allan o diwn a rhes o gantorion trist oedd mor bell o efelychu Elvis ag oedd Yuri Gagarin o gael ei ddewis yn arlywydd nesa'r Unol Daleithiau.

Un bora felly, efo'r freuddwyd o fod yn big-shot mor llipa â chynffon cath wlyb rhwng ei goesa (ac efo llai na $800 o arian Anti Sally ar ôl) yn hytrach na anelu'r Studebaker i'r chwith – er mwyn mynd i lawr Highway 85 i weld os oedd yna well grwpiau a chantorion yn Tuskegee, Macon County – dyma "Crazy" Luke Dober yn troi i'r dde.

Ac am adra.

Wrth i'r glaw chwipio'r sgrin, ac wrth i'r trefi a'r pentrefi a'r motels wibio heibio dyma "Crazy" Luke Dober yn sylweddoli nad oedd o byth am gael ei bum munud yn haul cynnes enwogrwydd fel ei hen ffrindiau, Little John and the Sweethearts a doedd o ddim am ddarganfod yr Elvis Presley nesa yn Lee County – nac yn Macon County chwaith. I ddeud y gwir, y ffordd oedd "Crazy" Luke Dober yn teimlo rŵan, roedd o'n eitha siŵr na fasa fo'n darganfod yr Elvis nesa tasa fo'n landio ar fonat y Studebaker y funud honno.

Ond, yn rhyfadd iawn, dyna'n union be ddigwyddodd.

Wrth yrru'n araf ar hyd prif stryd Marlonville (tre, neu bentre i fod yn fwy cywir, â 2,136 o bobol) dyma "Crazy" Luke Dober yn plygu drosodd i newid yr orsaf ar ei radio ac, yn ystod yr eiliad honno – pan wnaeth o dynnu ei lygaid oddi ar y lôn – dyma fo'n taro rwbath. Rwbath swmpus. Rwbath ddigon swmpus i greu tolc sylweddol yn hwd y Studebaker Commander. Am eiliad, wrth iddo fo dynnu'r car i'r ochor a'i barcio'n frysiog ar hanner y palmant, roedd "Crazy" Luke Dober yn meddwl falla'i fod o wedi taro ci, neu geffyl.

Ond wedyn, drwy'r glaw, dyma fo'n gweld siâp dyn. Dyn mawr. Deunaw stôn yn bendant. Neu fwy. Ugain? Beth bynnag, roedd swmp y gŵr yma yn amlwg wedi ei achub rhag unrhyw fath o niwed difrifol oherwydd rŵan roedd o'n codi ar ei draed ac yn twtio'i wallt fel tasa fo heb neud ddim byd gwaeth na baglu dros labrador.

"Hei," meddai "Crazy" Luke Dober, gan redeg draw ato'n syth (y peth dwytha oedd o angen rŵan – ar ben bob dim arall – oedd hwn yn ei siwio), "wyt ti'n iawn, Ffrind?"

"Yndw, dwi'n ocê."

"Nes i ddim dy weld di."

"Ti'n jocio wyt ti? Sut fedrat ti beidio fy ngweld? Y dyn mwya yn y dre – a'r unig un du!" Dyma fo'n ysgwyd ei ben mewn anghrediniaeth. "Mae rhan fwya o bobol o gwmpas y lle yma'n sylwi arna i'n syth!"

Am eiliad anghyfforddus roedd "Crazy" Luke Dober yn siŵr fod o mewn trwbwl go iawn. Doedd 'na neb arall o gwmpas. Neb i'w helpu tasa'r tarw o ddyn yma'n penderfynu troi arno a'i ladd. Roedd y glaw'n taro'r tarmac fel bwledi. Pwy fasa'n dewis mynd allan ar noson fel hon?

Efo'i galon fel pedal drwm bas dyma "Crazy" Luke Dober yn llyncu ei boer a thrio gwella'r sefyllfa. Roedd o wedi darllen am bobol yn cael eu lladd mewn trefi bach fel hyn. Trefi tawel. Efo jyst un car plisman.

"Hei, gwranda, ti'n siŵr dy fod ti'n ocê? Wyt ti isho i mi alw am ddoctor ne rwbath?"

"Na, dwi'm angen doctor. A beth bynnag, ti'n meddwl fod gen ddyn fel fi insiwrans meddygol? Jyst pasia hwnna i mi, wnei di?"

Roedd y gŵr diarth yn cyfeirio at gas gitar. Dyma "Crazy" Luke yn ei basio.

"Ti'n gerddor?"

"George Morton," medda'r gŵr mawr, gan estyn ei law rhydd a gwenu'n heintus. "Er, mae rhan fwya o bobol yn fy ngalw i'n 'Tiny'. Fel rhyw fath o jôc, ti'n gweld. Hei, pam na ddei di i 'ngweld i? Mae gen i gig heno. Dwi angen dipyn o gefnogaeth – wnes i golli'n job heddiw – wedyn dyma fi'n cael fy nharo i lawr gan boi dall mewn Studebaker. Ar ben hyn i gyd mae hi'n piso bwrw ac mae pawb call adra o flaen y teledu. Weithia dwi'n meddwl fod Iesu Grist wedi creu anlwc jyst er fy mwyn i."

"Ia, wel," meddai "Crazy" Luke Dober dan ei wynt. "Falla ddim jyst ti."

Roedd y Golden Bronco mor wahanol i'r Hollywood Bowl ag oedd Betws y Coed i Tokyo ond o leia roedd o dan do. Erbyn hyn roedd crys "Crazy" Luke Dober yn socian ac mor dynn â haen arall o groen, a doedd George "Tiny" Morton yn edrych fawr gwell. Roedd ei siwt fel tasa hi wedi crebachu rwsut – ac, wrth gwrs, mi oedd 'na res o rwygiadau arni a phatrymau Jackson Pollockaidd o fwd, baw a graean.

"Be uffar ddigwyddodd i chdi?" meddai'r perchennog. "Ti'n edrych fel shit!"

"Nath y boi yma fy nharo i efo'i gar."

Dyma'r perchennog yn edrych ar "Crazy" Luke Dober am eiliad cyn poeri mewn i bwcad a throi'n ôl at "Tiny".

"Wel, well i ti fynd i ganu. Mae dy gynulleidfa'n disgwl."

"Ia," meddai "Tiny", wrth edrych o gwmpas y Golden Bronco gwag, "hawdd gweld hynny."

Wrth sbio ar "Tiny" yn plygio ei gitar i'r amp gyda chlec amhroffesiynol, ac yna'n ymddiheurio, roedd disgwyliadau "Crazy" Luke Dober yn eitha isel. Y peth dwytha roedd o isho glywad oedd canwr gwael arall yn dinistrio rhai o glasuron R&B y dydd. Be oedd o isho go iawn rŵan oedd mynd adra, cael bath, wisgi a mynd i'w wely. Ond sut fedar o wrthod gwahoddiad gan rywun roedd o newydd ei daro? Fasa deud 'na' i "Tiny" yn anghwrtais – creulon, hyd yn oed. Na, y peth gora i'w neud oedd ordro Pepsi ac aros am ychydig – tair cân efalla – cyn sleifio i ffwrdd heb i neb sylwi (er fod hynny'n mynd i fod yn anodd mewn lle mor wag). Felly, efo'r Pepsi yn ei law dyma "Crazy" Luke yn troi i wynebu'r llwyfan...

... a chael ei syrfdanu.

Roedd George "Tiny" Morton yn seren. Mi oedd hyn yn amlwg i "Crazy" Luke hyd yn oed os oedd y tri person arall yn y Golden Bronco ddim yn medru gwerthfawrogi'r ffaith. Doedd "Crazy" Luke Dober ddim yn medru credu'r peth! Pam nad oedd y Golden Bronco yn orlawn a phawb yn neidio i fyny ac i lawr ac yn dawnsio'n wyllt i lais anhygoel a rhythmig George "Tiny" Morton? Pam nad oedd neb yn clapio ac yn neidio ar ben y bwrdd pŵl? Roedd ei ddawn mor naturiol. Ei lais mor ddwfn a chynoesol. Weithia, wrth iddo fo gyrraedd diwedd lein, roedd 'na ryw rathell gyntefig yn rhwygo o'i fron fel cri o galon dynoliaeth. Cri o galon America oedd hon. Cri oedd yn cynnig gobaith. Cri oedd yn dechrau fel sbarc ond oedd yn cynyddu nes iddi losgi drwy prysglwyni sych a diffrwyth diffeithwch y wlad fel fflamau efengylaidd a gwaredol.

Ai "Crazy" Luke Dober oedd yr unig berson i weld ac i adnabod hyn?

Ar ôl gorffen set tri chwarter awr aeth George "Tiny" Morton i'r bar, fel arfer, ac archebu gwydraid o root beer. Oedd ganddo fo ddeg munud cyn dechra'r ail set ond, yn ystod y deg munud hwnnw, (a chyn iddo fo gael cyfla i yfad y root beer) mi roedd o wedi arwyddo cytundeb efo Hit-State Records (cytundeb gafodd ei pharatoi yn frysiog ar gefn poster roedd "Crazy" Luke Dober wedi ei rwygo oddi ar wal y Golden Bronco). Wedyn, ymhen wythnos, roedd o'n gwrando yn ôl ar recordiad o "Please Be My Baby" o'i soffa yn 23009 Meadowville ac yn gwenu'n foddhaus wrth i'r bas bery i'r seinyddion grynu.

"Mae hon yn hit!" meddai "Crazy" Luke Dober, gan orfod gweiddi dros y gerddoriaeth. "Dwi'n deud 'tha chdi, George! Hit go iawn!"

"Wel, mae'n swnio'n dda, mae raid i mi gyfadda!"

Roedd ymateb cynnar WB-NBX yn Auburn yn hynod o frwdfrydig a chalonogol hefyd. Yn y gorffennol cafodd "Crazy" Luke Dober y teimlad fod y DJs lleol wedi chwarae recordiau Hit-State mewn cydymdeimlad a phiti, ond yn achos "Please Be My Baby" roedd yr ymateb yn hollol wahanol. Roedd y DJs i gyd yn heidio rownd y Dansette ac yn chwarae'r copi promo drosodd a throsodd, gan ddawnsio a chwerthin.

"Mae hon yn hit!" meddai Hube Long, un o DJ's mwya dylanwadol WB-NBX, gan daro "Crazy" Luke Dober ar ei gefn yn frawdgarol. "Pryd gawn ni chwarae hi ar y radio?"

"Unrhyw bryd lici di. Mae hi allan mewn wythnos – ar y 23ain."

"Hei," meddai Hube Long, ei ddannedd yn felyn a'i wynt yn drewi o Camels. "Dyna fydd dy ddiwrnod lwcus. Mae hon yn mynd i fod yn rif un!"

Doedd y ffôn yn 23009 Meadowville erioed wedi canu gymaint efo DJs o orsafoedd pell yn Efrog Newydd a Chicago yn mynnu copis promo o "Please Be My Baby". Erbyn hyn dim ond dau gant o gopïau oedd ar ôl i'w gwerthu i'r siopau, felly dyma "Crazy" Luke Dober yn cysylltu â'r ffatri yn Albertstown i ddyblu'r ordor. Jyst i fod yn saff dyma fo'n cysylltu â ffatri arall – ffatri fwy – yn Los Angeles i weld os fasa nhw'n medru delio efo'r niferoedd fasa'u hangen tasa 'Please Be My Baby' yn torri mewn i siartiau *Billboard*, fel roedd pawb yn proffwydo.

Un pnawn roedd rhywun o RCA Victor wedi galw yn gofyn cwestiyna am "Tiny" Morton (roedd "Crazy" Luke Dober wedi perswadio ei ddarpar seren i ollwng 'George' oherwydd ei fod o'n rhy hen ffasiwn) ond roedd perchennog Hit-State Records wedi mwynhau dweud wrth y big-shot o

L.A. fod Morton yn un o artistiaid y label o Meadowville a'i fod o ddim – ripît, ddim – ar gael!

Ar fore'r 22ain gysgodd "Crazy" Luke Dober yn hwyr. A pwy fedar feio'r boi? Roedd y misoedd ers iddo fo daro i mewn i Tiny Morton – yn llythrennol – wedi bod yn wyllt! Recordio, ordro a goruchwylio cynhyrchiad y sengl, teithio o gwmpas gorsafoedd radio lleol, delio â'r galwadau ffôn a'r llythyrau, wedyn ailordro copïau o'r sengl, paratoi datganiadau i'r wasg ac ailddrafftio cytundeb Hit-State Records efo "Tiny" Morton, jyst rhag ofn i RCA Victor alw eto. Wrth gwrs roedd "Crazy" Luke Dober yn berffaith fodlon gwerthu ei seren am ffortiwn i label fawr – yn union fel wnaeth Sam Phillips efo Elvis. Ond dim eto. Ddim tan fyddai'r pris wedi codi rhywfaint. Ddim tan fyddai 'Please Be My Baby' yn neg uchaf siart *Billboard*.

Y peth cynta wnaeth o oedd rhoi'r teciall ymlaen am goffi a chlicio'r radio, gan ddisgwyl clywed Hube Long ar WB-NBX yn chwarae'r gân ac yn mynnu fod pawb yn ei phrynu y bore wedyn pan fydda hi yn y siopau o'r diwedd.

Ond, na.

Y cyfan glywodd "Crazy" Luke Dober ar ei radio y bore hwnnw oedd rhyw ŵr diarth yn siarad yn eitha soniarus a thrist am rywbeth oedd wedi digwydd yn Texas.

Texas?

Be wnelo WB-NBX yn Auburn â Thexas?

Mewn dig dyma fo'n troi'r deial i WFFX yn Lanceton. Roedd y derbyniad braidd yn sâl ond yr un peth oedd y neges yma hefyd. Dau lais yn trafod Texas. Be goblyn oedd yn bod ar y byd? Pam nad oedd "Tiny" Morton i'w glywed yn bloeddio 'Please Be My Baby' i glustiau parod America? Pam nad oedd y DJs wedi cadw at eu gair? Mi oedd hon yn hit! Dyna be oedd pawb wedi'i ddeud!

Dyma'r ffôn yn canu.

"Hei," medda "Tiny" Morton, ei lais yn swnio'n eitha trwm a thrist am unwaith. "Ti 'di clywed y newyddion?"

"Dwi heb glywed dy gân di, mae hynna'n saff."

"Mae rhyw foi wedi saethu Kennedy yn Dallas."

Mae pawb yn America sydd dros 55 yn debygol o wybod yn union lle oeddan nhw pan glywson nhw'r newyddion fod Kennedy wedi cael ei ladd. Mi roedd "Crazy" Luke Dober yn ei stafell yn ei byjamas.

O fewn awr mi oedd o yn yr ardd efo tri chan gwag o Budweiser wrth ei draed. O fewn mis roedd y biliau am "Please Be My Baby" wedi cyrraedd.

O fewn tri mis roedd y Beatles wedi newid cerddoriaeth yn America am byth. O fewn pum mis roedd heddlu Lee County wedi tynnu corff gŵr yn ei dridegau canol o Afon Chattahoochee. Ebrill 3ydd, 1964.

Prin fod neb yn cofio lle roedda nhw fu farw "Crazy" Luke Dober.

"THE BEATLES ARE COMING!"

AN AFTERWORD

My dad may not have known Lloyd George but what do I care? He knew someone far cooler. Ritchie. Spoke to him many times in fact. During the late fifties, before I was born, my dad claimed that the two men developed something of a casual friendship over regular pints and sandwiches at the Garddfon Inn at Felinheli in Gwynedd (or Caernarvonshire as it was then). Despite their age differences (my dad was ten years older) they kind of clicked and the friendship only fizzled out because they both got promotions. My dad stopped being a rent collector for Gwyrfai Council and got himself a nice office job. Ritchie's promotion was a little more spectacular. He stopped working as a barman on the Liverpool ferry...

And became a Beatle.

Yes, my dad knew Ringo Starr. Or, at least, he knew Ritchie Starkey. John, Paul, George and Ritchie, there on the telly in his lounge, shaking their heads and screaming on the Royal Variety Performance with the Queen Mum rattling her fucking jewellery.

"Dwi'n nabod hwn!" said my dad. ("I know him!")

But my mum didn't believe him.

"Wrth gwrs dy fod ti!" ("Yes, of course you do.")

"No really. Cheese and pickle sandwiches and a pint of mild at the Garddfon. That's Ritchie!"

"Don't be silly," said my mum, "that's Ringo."

My dad was always something of a fibber. He once told me he'd invented salt.

"I had a chemistry set one Christmas," he said, "and I started playing with it. I did a few experiments and then, all of a sudden, all this stuff appeared. It was a completely new thing that no one had ever seen before. I decided to call it salt."

I was eight and sitting at the back of the car. We were driving along the coast road from Llandudno one windy Saturday afternoon and I was looking at the white-topped waves trying to see the giant horses that my dad had once said sometimes swam over from the Isle of Man.

"Well, I didn't know what to do," said my dad. "Your gran was frantic. All this salt was flowing down the stairs from my bedroom and it was almost covering up the sofa in the lounge! 'You've got to do something Selwyn!' she screamed. And so I did."

"What did you do dad?"

"I wrote to the Prime Minister. 'Dear Mister Heath,' I said. 'I've invented this stuff with my chemistry set and now there's mountains of it and I don't know what to do with it. My mum is going mad because it's now covered up the sofa and we can't find the cat. What can I do?' Well, naturally, the Prime Minister is a busy man. I didn't hear anything for weeks, by which time we'd moved out of the house and were forced to live above the coalshed in the garden. But the letter came back from 10 Downing Street eventually."

"What did it say dad?"

"Mr Heath told me the best thing to do was throw it all into the sea. So that's what I did. And you see son, that's why the sea is so salty. I did that. With my chemistry set."

My mum turned round and winked at me. Yes, my dad was a fibber. I believed that story about the salt for years until I discovered the sad, and rather prosaic truth.

He never told me about Ringo until I was in my twenties and had become something of a Beatles nut. By then my dad had stopped telling tall tales about giant horses from the Isle of Man and chemistry sets. We were in the Garddfon Inn having one of our rather awkward father and son chats whilst I was back from university. Breaking one of the silences he casually dropped the story like a grenade.

"Of course this was where I used to talk to Ringo."

I believed him. I think it was because pop music meant nothing to him. He was just the most unswingiest cat in town. Squarer than a square box of cubes in a huge square-shaped warehouse on a square planet in the constellation of Square. He just didn't get it. Not just pop music but *any* kind of music. Beethoven, Bach, Beatles or Bechet. It was all a racket to him. He called it all 'jazz' and often spat it out as if 'jazz' was a swear word. So he didn't mention the 'Ringo anecdote' to impress me because he himself wasn't impressed by it. He only knew that I was obsessed by the Beatles and that it might be of passing interest to me that he'd once known their future drummer. That was all. *Of passing interest?* Was he kidding??

What on earth could they have talked about?

Not rock and roll, that was for sure. My dad didn't know his Elvis from his elbow. Not even the cinema (my mum told me years later that my dad had only been to see one film ever and that he'd fallen asleep in the Majestic in Caernarfon, snoring loudly and embarrassing my mum so much that she never went with him to the cinema again.) Football perhaps? My dad had been a promising amateur goalie and had even been for a trial with Bolton Wanderers (who wanted him but because he was always a cautious soul who felt a duty to look after his widowed mum he declined and took a steady job instead) but I knew that none of the Beatles had ever been into sport. Women? My dad was a handsome sod in his youth (far better looking than anyone in the Beatles – except for George perhaps) but he was never a cad. Beer? He liked a drink but would just as easily have supped tea. Perhaps my dad explained the rigours of the ancient Welsh poetic form of the cynghanedd to him? Poetry was a passion and his ambition was always to win the crown at the National Eisteddfod. Perhaps Ritchie nodded politely as my dad scribbled down algebraic internal rhyme systems down on a ripped beer mat. Probably not.

The irritating thing was that my dad – my dad who *knew* Ringo – couldn't remember. And that's probably why I believed him. There was no bullshit this time. A bullshitter would have seen the look on my face and, encouraged, he would have spun several tall tales and a Beatles nut like me would have privately punched holes in the chronology just as easily as Joe Frazier would have punched through a cobweb.

"You knew Ringo," I said. "That's amazing."

"Yes, very polite he was."

He placed his pint carefully down on the beer mat, wiped the side of his mouth with a handkerchief and turned to me.

"Did I ever tell you about the phone call?"

By 1967 my dad was a mature student doing a teacher training course at the Normal College in Bangor. He was still writing poetry and by then he'd managed to win quite a few Eisteddfod chairs for his work although the Big Dream was still to win the crown at the National Esiteddfod and become a 'Prifardd' (a bardic poet). To supplement his income he'd begun working part-time as a researcher/journalist with the Welsh independent TV service at the time TWW. Conveniently, they had a small office in Bangor in a cavernous old shell of a building called Caxton House which had once been a thriving printing works (don't go looking for it, today it's a branch of Boots).

One afternoon the phone rang in Mr Pritchard's office. It echoed like St Paul's cathedral. My dad jumped. He'd been reading a poetry journal with his feet up on the table. Nothing ever happened in the Bangor TWW office. 'Things that happen' were the prerogative of the Cardiff office – all dolly birds and cigarette smoke and clacking typewriters down in Swinging Pontcanna. Bangor was like a sleepy Mexican town in a western by comparison.

My dad pushed back his sombrero.

Mr Pritchard was out. (He always insisted on the 'Mr' because he was the boss. And because he was a hard-nosed, old-school bastard). My dad was terrified of him. He'd thunder out of his office and yell at everyone like Popeye after a fix of spinach, his sleeves rolled up as if news was something to actually fight.

Only, of course, there was hardly ever any news.

A minor road accident on the coast road perhaps. A near-miss at RAF Valley on Anglesey. They normally got one of the lower slots on the regional news – the filmed report being taken down by courier along the winding A470 from Bangor to

Cardiff by a reckless driver who overtook farmers and lorries like Jim Clark to get the film processed in time for transmission – but never the top story. Like I say, all the top stories happened in Cardiff. Nothing ever happened in Bangor.

But now the phone was ringing.

Mr Pritchard had left my dad in charge. Grudgingly it had to be said. Mr Pritchard had no time for part-timers. Especially part-timers who wrote poetry. But no one else had been available that day and the dental appointment couldn't be moved so needs must.

"Look after the office," he'd barked.

"Of course Mr Pritchard."

My dad was in his thirties but, somehow, Mr Pritchard had the knack of making him feel ten years old. The grumpy boss gave him the once-over and made a disparaging sound from the back of his throat like John Wayne about to use a spitoon. He grabbed his hat and left, his shoes stamping the stairs as if they were cockroaches.

Now the phone was ringing.

And it wouldn't stop.

How my dad wished there was someone else around to take responsibility. Someone else to open the door to Mr Pritchard's office and answer the call. But there wasn't. It was up to him.

Putting down the poetry book my dad tentatively walked across to the office. Once inside the phone seemed even more insistent. Phones never usually rang for this long. There must have been a bigger than usual accident on the coast road. Or maybe one of the planes at RAF Valley had caught fire.

"Helo, TWW. Sut fedra'i helpu?"

There was a pause on the other side. Then a puzzled voice.

"Is that TWW in Bangor?"

The voice sounded posh. My dad switched to English.

"Yes. How can I help?"

"The Beatles are coming."

"I'm sorry?"

"They've just left Euston. They should be there in about four hours."

"The who?"

There was an agitated sigh on the other side.

"That is TWW isn't it?"

"Yes, but..."

"Look, they're going to be up in Bangor by the end of the afternoon. They're going to Normal College with the Maharishi. Do you understand?"

"Yes but..."

"Should be long enough for you to get crew and some reporters together."

The stranger with the posh voice hung up and my dad held on to the receiver like a dead pet. When Mr Pritchard arrived back from the dentist half an hour later my dad told him the Beatles were coming. There had been a call, he said. From London. The Beatles were coming to Normal College. Mr Pritchard's face went as red as Mars. He couldn't speak. It was probably a combination of the dentist's injection and sheer fury that my dad had been taken in by such an obvious hoax. He went into his office and slammed the door so hard my dad half-expected the frosted glass with Mr Pritchard's name on it to smash into a million pieces.

Four hours later the Beatles' train pulled in to Bangor station.

I can't imagine two more different world's than the ones which belonged to my dad and the Fab Four, and yet there was a tenuous connection. This is probably what sub-consciously made me wonder what would have happened had John, Paul, George and Ritchie (sorry, *Ringo*) sought out such a world such as his, a completely different world, at the height of their fame. Two different worlds colliding, neither truly understanding the other. Perhaps my dad was the model for Tom Morris. Not that my dad knew anything about pigeons of course. I simply tried to pick something as far removed from Beatledom as I could think of and tried to leave it teetering on the brink of plausibility. The band were notoriously faddish after all so why not pigeons? I tried to make it as convincing as I could, even checking for blank dates in Mark Lewisohn's brilliant *Beatles Chronicle* and trying to fit the events in accordingly. I love reading books about the Beatles. I have shelves and shelves full of them – and, in my own way I suppose I wanted to write my own (my dad always told me I should) but, being essentially a lazy sod, I just couldn't be arsed to do the research so I just made it up and had a laugh. My only piece of solid research was when I phoned up a genuine pigeon fancier to get some information about what they actually fed their birds. I think he thought I was a bit mad but he was very sweet and gave me all that stuff about Willsbridge which serves to give the tale at least a wispy tang of authenticity.

David Hepworth may well be correct when he says that the more we learn about the Beatles the less surprised we become at the sheer outlandishness of certain elements of their story. Perhaps the second and third volumes of Mark Lewisohn's comprehensive biography will reveal that all of this *did* actually happen! Truth is often weirder than fiction when it comes to the Beatles. Of course, being a tenacious seeker, Mr Lewisohn may well discover that it wasn't actually my dad who took the call that day and that there wasn't a real Mr Pritchard. Well, I'll spare him some valuable research hours on that score at least. I made Mr Pritchard up. But the rest is true.

Take it from the son of a born fibber.

My dad did eventually achieve his life's ambition. He won the crown at the National Eisteddfod at Llanrwst in 1989. I was there and even though the Eisteddfod never meant that much to me I knew that, for him, it was worth a thousand 'jazz' groups.

He passed away in 2011 and I dedicate this volume to his memory.

IMPOSTOR

This is not you because you don't work
anymore. Hands that once caused crowds
to roar in derby matches – flicking
balls like flies over the bar – now struggle
with a fork. That chest which swelled
to face the cavalry stampede of strikers
groans at all the air still left in the world.
Legs which booted the ball miles behind
enemy lines now buckle like wiry twigs.

THE BEATLES IN TONYPANDY

We sit in the car listening to the sea
and the football results. Bolton wanted you
once. You could have played in the
Matthews final but you stayed behind.
Old enough to kick you taught me the goalie's trade –
dragging lines in the grass with your boot
to show where the posts were. Making
your body big. Yours has shrunk.
I never got a ball past you, now
I could score all day. You smile and
the tutti-frutti dribbles like Charlton down
your cheek. I flick a tissue. Wipe it away.

www.ingramcontent.com/pod-product-compliance
Lightning Source LLC
Chambersburg PA
CBHW071438080526
44587CB00014B/1907